THE FRANCISCAN VISION
AND
THE GOSPEL OF JOHN

The San Damiano Crucifix

Francis and John

Creation and John

MICHAEL D. GUINAN, O.F.M.

VOLUME FOUR
THE FRANCISCAN HERITAGE SERIES

CFIT/ESC-OFM
2006

**This pamphlet is the fourth in
The Franciscan Heritage Series
sponsored by the
Commission on the Franciscan Intellectual Tradition
of the English-speaking Conference of the Order of Friars Minor
(CFIT/ESC-OFM)**

General Editor

Joseph P. Chinnici, O.F.M.

Assistant Editor

Elise Saggau, O.S.F.

Previous titles in this series:

*The Franciscan Intellectual Tradition: Tracing Its Origins and
Identifying Its Central Components* (2003) Kenan B. Osborne, O.F.M.

*A Franciscan View of Creation:
Learning to Live in a Sacramental World* (2003) Ilia Delio, O.S.F.

*The Franciscan View of the Human Person:
Some Central Elements* (2005) Dawn M. Nothwehr, O.S.F.

ISBN: 1-57659-2030

Library of Congress Control Number: 2006923596

Printed and bound in the United States of America
BookMasters, Inc.
Ashland, Ohio

TABLE OF CONTENTS

GENERAL EDITOR'S INTRODUCTION

The Franciscan Vision and the Gospel of John by Professor Michael D. Guinan, O.F.M., marks the fourth offering in the Franciscan Heritage Series (FHS) sponsored by the Commission for the Retrieval of the Franciscan Intellectual Tradition (CFIT) of the English Speaking Conference of the Order of Friars Minor. Professor Guinan brings to this interpretation a wealth of knowledge in scripture studies and biblical spirituality. Professor of Old Testament and Semitic Languages at the Franciscan School of Theology, Berkeley, California, this well-known Franciscan priest unites, in his teachings and in his specialized writings, recent trends in the study of the Pentateuch and Wisdom literature with fundamental themes in the Franciscan theological tradition. This present effort makes a distinctive and much needed bridge between the best of contemporary scholarship on the Wisdom traditions of the Old Testament, the Gospel of John and the vernacular tradition of Francis's own theology expressed in his writings and portrayed for the community in the San Damiano Cross. Accompanied by a CD-Rom presentation of the crucifix, this volume correlates a central image-text of community formation with Johannine insights into the mystery of creation, incarnation, glory and ministry.

With great pleasure and gratitude, the sponsors of CFIT offer this reflection to a wider public. We hope it will present, in an accessible and exciting form, some central elements of the Franciscan theological vision. We imagine it being used in college classrooms, in parish adult education programs, in Secular Fraternity gatherings and in various community meetings. The depth of the presentation will be plumbed only through a process of gazing, studying, conversing, praying and acting. Our intellectual and affective work, as both Bonaventure and Scotus would argue, exists for the sake of personal, communal and social transformation. As Professor Guinan indicates in his conclusion, people today long *to see* the image-text of a living God. Perhaps, like Clare herself, readers and practitioners of the Franciscan Gospel life, gazing upon the cross with informed minds and open hearts, might become transformed into the "image of the Godhead itself" so as to enable others *to read* and *to become* the true "glory" of the love of God and neighbor in our twenty-first century. May the Holy Spirit guide us in this task.

Making Connections

One of the chief purposes of the CFIT project is not only to expose the riches of the intellectual tradition but also to retrieve it in such a way that it might become available to disciples of Christ and members of his Body in the twenty-first century. At times, this retrieval may require that the intellectual forms of the scholastic heritage give way to modern interpretive categories inherited from linguistic philosophy, sociology, psychology, feminist studies, ritual analysis and recent historical interpretation. While remaining faithful to key intuitions and insights, both in the spiritual experience of Francis and Clare and in the philosophical and theological expressions of the tradition in the schools, the project's purpose is to bridge the past and the present. In this way, we hope to establish historical resonance between two distinct eras. Such a dialogue and exchange can only illuminate both the understanding of the tradition and its contemporary deepening and application.

The reader can see in the present volume that Dr. Guinan has traversed the territory well and in doing so has given us a path for the future. In an exemplary way, he has taken a traditional icon of the community, one not even generated by a Franciscan, aligned it with an analysis of Francis's own writings and interfaced both the icon and the person with contemporary Scriptural interpretation. In a global world, this is not simply the repetition of a tradition that has seen its time, but the retrieval of a living tradition in the Church and society of today. The reader is encouraged to meditate on the icon of the cross through the eyes of Francis's images and through the overarching themes of John's own Gospel passion. To unpack its full richness, such a task will demand time and thought. This brief Introduction indicates only a few ways in which this overly rich and deceptively simple reflection might be expanded.

The text merely hints at the asceticism of vision that this tradition imposes. What is viewed with the eyes is meant to transform the heart and the mind so that one might see, interpret and act in the world through the loving power of God, Creator, Redeemer and

Sanctifier. In a world shaped by pictures, what images educate our affections into the project of the Great Commandment? As God becomes the object of our contemplative vision, we become more deeply the image of our Creator God. (Cf. David Chidester, *Word and Light, Seeing, Hearing and Religious Discourse*, 1992). As we see the world with Christ's open gaze, perhaps the sight of our neighbor's suffering washes us with tears of repentance and compassion. The work of justice calls us forward. But first we must *see* with the contemplative eye: "Therefore open your eyes, alert your spiritual ears, unlock your lips, and apply your heart so that in all creation you may see, hear, praise, love and adore, magnify and honor your God lest the entire world rise up against you" (Bonaventure, *Itinerarium*, 1:15).

In the light of what is offered here, we can now simultaneously retrieve the San Damiano cross and recognize the ethical stance of responsibility for the environment that the "cosmos as temple" demands. Before us also loom the ecclesiological dimensions of the Johannine interpretation of the "abbreviated Word" of Christ present in glory in the community of believers. Does the blood of Christ flowing down upon each member of the community of penitents at the foot of the cross not push us, as it did Bonaventure, towards recognizing the diversity of gifts in the one Body of Christ? Can we make the connection between our daily or weekly Eucharistic practice and this cosmic vision of a Christic universe? To do any of this we need training. By focusing the "eye of our heart" through the images presented here and understanding them intellectually through the scholarship of today, we open up the deep relationship between prayer and action, mind and heart, personal transformation and mission in the world, the sacraments of the Church and our own contemporary exploration of the universe.

Most notably, the striking references to the continuing work of God in creation through Wisdom establish a biblical base for Franciscan evangelization. Our work is directed to the revelation of the presence of the Word in places where before it was not recognized. Perhaps this is what happened to Francis when he worked mercy among the lepers; perhaps his experience of "sweetness" was the discovery of Incarnate Wisdom still dwelling with and accompanying the poor. Perhaps he *saw* that same Spirit of Wisdom at work in Clare when she considered as "great delights . . . deprivation, poverty, hard work, trial, or the shame or contempt of the

world." Observing this, Francis "rejoiced in the Lord," much as Elizabeth did when Mary visited her (*Testament of Clare*, 27-28). The ethical consequences: Francis embraced her as his companion. Perhaps
confidence in God's continuing work in creation enabled Francis to
describe his preferred posture among non-believers in these terms:

> As for the brothers who go, they can live spiritually among
> the Saracens and nonbelievers in two ways. One way is not
> to engage in arguments or disputes but to be subject *to every*
> *human creature for God's sake* and to acknowledge that they
> are Christians. The other way is to announce the Word of
> God, when they see it pleases the Lord, in order that [unbe-
> lievers] may believe in almighty God, the Father, the Son,
> and the Holy Spirit, the Creator of all, the Son, the Redeemer
> and Savior, and be baptized and become Christians because
> *no one can enter the kingdom of God without being reborn of water*
> *and the Holy Spirit* (ER 16:5-7).

Following in the footsteps of Francis, our method of evangelization is one of presence and affirmation, persuasion and recognition,
seeing and incorporating the neighbor as sister or brother: "It is likewise evident how wide is the illuminative way and how in everything which is perceived or known God Himself lies hidden within"
(Bonaventure, *On Retracing the Arts to Theology*, 26). Gazing on this
Wisdom Cross has personal, ethical, social, ecclesial and political
consequences for how we choose to live and witness in the world!

The Uniqueness of the Franciscan Vision

The San Damiano Crucifix, meditation on the Word of God in Scripture and the evangelical life of Francis and Clare are at the heart of
the Franciscan vision. Professor Guinan shows us the significance
of the Gospel of John as a directive force, particularly in its key images of Word, Lamb, Good Shepherd and the One Who Washes Feet.
It is also important to note that this exposition points to one of the
deepest realities that make the Franciscan vision of the Christian
Catholic life unique in the Church. In no other spiritual tradition do
we find a central emphasis placed upon the Gospel passage of the
new family of Christ. In contrast to the monastic model of the com-

munity of believers described in Acts 2:42-47, 3:32-35 (an image dominant in the Gregorian reform and in the tradition, but one not even
referred to by Francis), the Johannine community of disciples pic-
tured at the foot of the San Damiano Cross places at the center of the
Franciscan intellectual vision the scene presented in the Synoptic
accounts:

> His mother and his brothers arrived, and as they stood out-
> side they sent word to him to come out. The crowd seated
> around him told him: "Your mother and your brothers and
> sisters are outside asking for you." He said in reply, "Who
> are my mother and my brothers?" And gazing around him
> at those seated in the circle he continued: "These are my
> mother and my brothers. Whoever does the will of God is
> brother and sister and mother to me" (Cf. Mk. 3:31-35, Mt.
> 12:46-50, Lk. 8:19-21).

> Near the cross of Jesus there stood his mother, his mother's
> sister, Mary the wife of Clopas, and Mary Magdalene. See-
> ing his mother there with the disciple whom he loved, Jesus
> said to his mother, "Woman, there is your son." In turn, he
> said to the disciple, "There is your mother." From that hour
> onward the disciple took her into his care (Jn. 19:25-27).

This fraternity of friends is constituted by those for whom Christ
gave up his life (Jn. 15:13)—male and female, Jew and Gentile, single
and married, old and young, well placed and lowly, invited together
into the very life of God. It comes from the creative and redemptive
work of Christ as he breathes out the Spirit on those willing to hear
the word of God and act upon it. As Christ's disciples, they become
mother, brother and sister not only to him but to each other. What is
created here is the fundamental reality of a Church marked by ma-
ternal, fraternal and sororal relationships. The image is meant to be
a counterweight to other styles of leadership and governance, to
complementary but alternate approaches to pastoral care. In the society of the times, it highlights the "law of reciprocity" and
relationality that guides a Franciscan sociology and a Franciscan
ecclesiology. Only a love willing to give itself for others can establish this community of persons.

Both Francis and Clare call attention to this image and its implications for the Christian vocation in the Church and the world. They add the spousal dimension, joining the person to the Holy Spirit, making him or her a "temple." Most famous of all is the passage from the *Earlier Exhortation*:

> We are spouses when the faithful soul is joined by the Holy Spirit to our Lord Jesus Christ. We are brothers to Him when we do the *will of the Father who is in heaven*. We are mothers when we carry Him in our heart and body through a divine love and a pure and sincere conscience and give birth to Him through a holy activity which must shine as an example before others (1LtF 8-10).

Clare refers to the images of sister, spouse and mother at the heart of the vocation in her letters to Agnes of Prague (1LAg 12, 24; 3LAg1, 4LAg4). For both Clare and Francis, the *imitatio mariae* (imitation of Mary) is the corollary to the *sequi Christi* (the following of Christ). Daily they pray, in the *Office of the Passion*, perhaps imaging to themselves the San Damiano Crucifix:

> Holy Virgin Mary, among the women born into the world, there is no one like you. *Daughter* and *servant* of the most high and supreme King and of the Father in heaven, *Mother* of our most holy Lord Jesus Christ, *Spouse* of the Holy Spirit, pray for us (Antiphon 1-3).

This sense of relational connection—the creation under God of a new kinship group not based on race, property, money, social status and power but on the free consent of anyone who chooses to do penance—permeates the entire vision of Francis and Clare for themselves, their Church and their society. The project of universal kinship stands in stark contrast to the economic and political consortia that dominated Assisi. (Cf. Arnaldo Fortini, *Francis of Assisi*, Chapter 2.)

Bonaventure will follow up on the uniqueness of this spiritual experience and social project in numerous writings. The *Itinerarium* (1-4) will speak about the presence of God in all creatures, the human being as the image of God and the soul as daughter, spouse and temple. The formational structure of this work will be directed to the furtherance of peace. The *Five Feasts of the Child Jesus* will develop a simple liturgical pedagogy designed to create a society of friends, a new type of consortium. Receiving the Word of God, the soul with Mary

> begins to flee the company of those with minds set on earthly things and desires the friendship of those with hearts set on heavenly things. It begins to take care of Elizabeth, that is, to look to those who are enlightened by divine wisdom and ardently inflamed by love.[1]

The *Commentary on Luke*, which has now been made available in English through the scholarship of Robert J. Karris, O.F.M., calls specific attention to the vocation of the Christian who receives this new world created by the Word of God:

> And note that he calls the listeners *mothers* in so far as they engender others through teaching, according to what Galatians 4:19 says: "My dear children, with whom I am in labor again, until Christ is formed in you."—He calls them brothers in that they are generated by the word and become sons of God, according to what the Psalmist says: "I will declare your name to my brothers" (21.23). As Hebrews 2:11 has: "He is not ashamed to call them brothers."[2]

So what do we have here? An image that shapes identity; . . . an illumination from the writings of Francis and Clare of Assisi; . . . a *lectio divina* by a contemporary Scripture scholar; . . . some theological insights of Bonaventure. Connecting the dots is what CFIT is all about.

The Franciscan Intellectual Tradition Project

In March 2001, the English-speaking Conference, Order of Friars Minor, undertook an initiative for the contemporary retrieval of the Franciscan Intellectual Tradition. Composed of the leaders of the provinces and other entities of England, Ireland, Canada and the United States, the Conference established an inter-obediential commission to facilitate the coordination and networking of various publications and popular initiatives that were already taking place throughout the English-speaking world.

As one of its first initiatives, this Commission for the Retrieval of the Franciscan Intellectual Tradition (CFIT) composed and published a strategic five-year plan and working document on the major themes of the theological and social vision. These initial plans and enunciation of the vision are available at website CFIT–ESC–OFM.org. The initiative has taken specific shape through the publication of the academic papers of an annual symposium at the Washington Theological Union, which to date has produced significant reflections in five major areas: *The Franciscan Intellectual Tradition* (2001), *Franciscan Identity and Postmodern Culture* (2002), *Franciscans and Creation* (2003), *Franciscans and the Church Today* (2004) and *Franciscans and the Scriptures: Living the Word of God* (2005).

The Heritage Series, now numbering four volumes, is designed to communicate the tradition in a shorter, more accessible and popular form for use in small groups and study clubs. A longer description of the CFIT project may be found in the Introduction to the first three volumes of the Heritage Series. All the publications are available through the Franciscan Institute, St. Bonaventure, New York. Formational work within and without the Franciscan family, networking among colleges and universities, the coordination of publishing, the translation of volumes in the Heritage Series into French and Spanish and the development of popular forms of communication through the use of technology and print media have been other parts of CFIT's beginning activity.

This program of spiritual, intellectual and pastoral renewal has now been elevated into the rank of a Secretariat of the Conference and projected to continue for another five years through 2011. Inquiries may be sent to members of the core commission: Father Joseph P. Chinnici, O.F.M., Franciscan School of Theology, 1712 Euclid Ave., Berkeley, California 94708; Sister Margaret Carney, President, or Brother Edward Coughlin, O.F.M., St. Bonaventure University, St. Bonaventure, New York, 14778.

Joseph P. Chinnici, O.F.M.
Franciscan School of Theology
Berkeley, California
February, 2006

NOTES

[1]Timothy J. Johnson, *Five Feasts*, in *Bonaventure, Mystic of God's Word*, Second ed. (St. Bonaventure, NY: Franciscan Institute Publications, 2005) 1:2, p. 141

[2]See Robert J. Karris, O.F.M.,*Commentary on the Gospel of Luke*, Part1, 8.32, Works of St. Bonaventure VIII (St. Bonaventure, NY: Franciscan Institute Publications, 2001, 684-85.

ABBREVIATIONS

Writings of Francis and Early Sources

FA:ED	*Francis of Assisi: Early Documents*. 3 volumes, ed. Regis J. Armstrong, O.F.M. Cap., J.A. Wayne Hellmann, O.F.M. Conv., William J. Short, O.F.M. (New York: New City Press, 1999, 2000, 2001). Citations will give the volume number, followed by the page number.

Writings of Francis

Adm	The Admonitions
BlL	A Blessing for Brother Leo
ER	The Earlier Rule (*Regula non bullata*)
LR	The Later Rule (*Regula bullata*)
1Frag	Fragments of Worchester Manuscript
1LtF	The First Letter to the Faithful (The Earlier Exhortation to the Brothers and Sisters of Penance)
2LtF	The Second Letter to the Faithful (The Later Admonition and Exhortation to the Brothers and Sisters of Penance)

LtOrd   A Letter to the Entire Order

PrH   The Praises to be said at all the Hours

PrOF   A Prayer Inspired by the Our Father

Early Biographical Sources

1C   The Life of St. Francis by Thomas of Celano

2C   The Second Life of Francis by Thomas of Celano (The Remembrance of the Desire of a Soul)

L3C   The Legend of the Three Companions

LMj   The *Legenda Major* (Major Legend) by St. Bonaventure

Other Sources

CBQ   *The Catholic Biblical Quarterly*

Gospel of John   Raymond E. Brown, *The Gospel According to John I-XII*, Anchor Bible, 29 (Garden City, NY: Doubleday, 1966). This is cited as volume 1.

     The Gospel According to John XIII-XXI, Anchor Bible, 29A (Garden City, NY: Doubleday, 1970). This is cited as volume 2.

The Teacher   Norbert Nguyen Van-Kanh, O.F.M., *The Teacher of His Heart: Jesus Christ in the Thought and Writings of St. Francis*, Franciscan Pathways (St.Bonaventure, NY: The Franciscan Institute, 1994).

PART ONE
AUTHOR'S INTRODUCTION

I remember (barely) when I got my first pair of glasses. I could suddenly see things I had either not seen before, or had seen but had forgotten—like the edges of leaves or the writing on signs in the distance. This was brought back to me when I had to get bifocals . . . and then trifocals! Again, I saw things sharply I had not noticed for a while, things far off and things close up. Whether far off or nearby, our vision sometimes fades, and we need to sharpen things up.

Something similar often happens in our spiritual lives. We go along our usual ways, engaged in our everyday, normal activities; then, without really noticing it, our vision begins to get fuzzy and hazy, and we do not see things as clearly. And this is too bad because spirituality is above all a question of vision.

How do we *see* God? How do we *see* the world? How do we *see* ourselves as human beings in relation to both God and the world? To sharpen our vision, we return to our story, as Christians and as Franciscans, and try to perceive it with new eyes.

As Franciscans, we go to the writings of Francis and Clare and the early writings about them. As Christians, we go to the Scriptures, Old and New Testaments, and especially to the Gospel stories. In both instances, we also look to the traditions that develop from them.

In the New Testament, each of the writings looks at Jesus and his work and meaning in a distinctive way. Within the overall unity of the early Christian witness, we find a diversity of "visions of Christ." Within these, the Johannine literature—the Gospel and Letters of John—are especially distinctive.[1]

While it used to be fairly common to see St. Francis as especially influenced by the Synoptic Gospels (Matthew, Mark and Luke), more recent study, based on the critical edition of his writings prepared by Kajetan Esser in 1978,[2] has shown how much St. Francis was indebted to and immersed in the Johannine vision.[3] In this volume of

1

the Franciscan Heritage series, we will introduce three aspects of this vision.

In Part Two, we will take a close look at the San Damiano Crucifix. It is rare to find a Franciscan place without a copy of this cross. In both a popular and a technical sense, it can be called a central Franciscan icon. In a popular sense, an icon is "a person or thing regarded as a representative symbol of something" (*New Oxford American Dictionary*). Our study will try to clarify just what that "something" is.

But it is an icon also in the more technical sense of "a painting of Christ or another holy figure, typically in a traditional style on wood, venerated and used as an aid to devotion in the Byzantine and other Eastern Churches." In the Eastern Christian tradition, icons are not just decorative art, but have a sacramental function. They are doors opening onto sacred space and time. God is experienced not only as truth and love, but also as beauty. Icons belong to the tradition of cataphatic prayer, in which a full use of the imagination and senses is put at the service of prayer. An icon is theology in a visually dense way in which everything counts. Each detail can and must be meditated on and prayed over.[4]

While it can justly be called a Franciscan icon, however, the San Damiano Cross is not a "Franciscan cross." As the Franciscan movement spread in the centuries after the death of Francis of Assisi, its focus on the humanity of Christ contributed to the development of crucifixes that portrayed more the suffering human body of Jesus.[5] The painting on the San Damiano Cross, generally placed around 1100 A.D., reflects a Syro-Byzantine style. Byzantine influence had been felt in Italy at least since the 550s when, under the emperor Justinian, Ravenna became part of the Byzantine empire; but Syrian monasteries were found in the Umbrian valley (where Assisi is located) in the centuries just before St. Francis. These may provide the background for the cross.

Almost all commentators on the San Damiano Crucifix agree that the key to interpreting its details lies in the Gospel of John. Surprisingly though, none of them applies this key consistently, being satisfied instead to point out a feature here, a feature there. In this study, we will examine the Crucifix, step by step, in the light of the Johannine Gospel.[6]

In Part Three, we will turn our attention to the writings of St. Francis and present some of the evidence that the Gospel of John was for him a major source of inspiration. This will appear especially in the favorite images of Jesus Francis often draws upon.

In Part Four, we will take a close look at the Prologue of John's gospel and its relationship to our understanding of creation. This is, of course, a large subject. Here our interest will be to draw on some aspects of contemporary biblical scholarship in order to clarify the background of Francis's view of creation. We will not argue that Francis understood the gospel passage explicitly in the way we propose, but rather that his relationship to creation is perfectly at home in the Johannine sacramental vision of the world.

In a brief work such as this, we can do no more than point in some directions. Other possible areas of influence could also be explored. One which comes right to mind would be the similarity between the Johannine view of each disciple gifted and led by the Holy Spirit and Francis's view of and respect for the gifted uniqueness of each individual. But I hope that what we have presented here might inspire and motivate us to a deeper and clearer appreciation of the vision of John in the New Testament and of the vision of Francis of Assisi.

PART TWO
THE SAN DAMIANO CRUCIFIX [1][7]

Near the beginning of his conversion, St. Francis used to pray in the small chapel of San Damiano, a short distance down the hill from Assisi. [2, 2a, 3, 4, 5] One day, according to the sources, Christ spoke to him from the cross: "Francis, go, repair my house, which, as you see, is falling completely to ruin."[8] Some time later, when Clare and her early followers lived at San Damiano, the crucifix undoubtedly was a focus of their meditation and reflection. When the body of St. Clare was moved to the new basilica on the site of the old Church of San Giorgio in 1260, the cross apparently was taken too, and it can be seen there to this day. [6]

Our study of the cross will proceed in three steps. [7] Taking our cues from the relative sizes of the figures, we will begin with the large and central figure of Christ on the cross; then we will move to the mid-sized community of disciples gathered under his arms; finally, we will look at the small figures located at the bottom, along the sides and at the top of the Cross.

The Figure of Jesus [8]

We will begin at the top of the figure and work our way down, commenting on specific items. Then, at the end, we will make a more general observation.

The Inscription

Since crucifixion was a very public form of execution and meant to be a deterrent, it was common that the specific crime being punished was named. All four of the gospels mention an inscription doing this, but, interestingly, no two of them are the same. [9]

- This is Jesus, the King of the Jews (Mt 27:37)
- The King of the Jews (Mark 15:26)
- This is the King of the Jews (Luke 23:38)
- Jesus of Nazareth, the King of the Jews (John 19:19)

5

We are told that it was written in Hebrew, Latin and Greek (John 19:20). The Latin form would have been *Jesus Nazarenus Rex Judaeorum.* [9a] Taking only the first letters, we get the abbreviation "INRI," which has become the form most familiar on our crucifixes. And it is this form, occurring precisely only in John, that we have on our cross.[9] [10] In John's Gospel, when Jesus was brought before Pilate, their conversation dealt with Jesus as King and the meaning of his kingship (John 18:28-19:16). When the chief priests objected to Pilate about the inscription, he replied: "What I have written, I have written" (John 19:21-22). The inscription acknowledges Jesus for what he truly is, a King.

The Face [11]

Eyes wide open, Jesus' face looks out peacefully. The crown of thorns (Mark 15:17; Mt 27:28-29; John 19:2) is conspicuously missing. In its place, the head of Jesus is encircled with a halo of glory. Contrary to our usual expectations, though, this halo is not behind the head of Jesus (as it is with the figures under his arms), but in front of it; the completion of its circle can be seen under the chin of Jesus.[10] [11a] We can notice how the halo effectively darkens the face of Jesus when compared with his upper body and arms.

A recurring theme in the Gospel of John is that in Jesus, we have seen the "glory of God." "And the Word became flesh and lived among us, and we have seen his glory" (1:14); "Jesus did this, the first of his signs, in Cana of Galilee, and revealed his glory" (2:11). Jesus' death on the cross is the hour of his glorification (12:23).

The "glory of God" image has deep roots in the Old Testament. The presence of God is often manifested in the form of a dark cloud with flashes of lightning in it. It is as if the light of God's presence is so overwhelming that the cloud covers God's presence and protects us from the full force of it. Thus, when the Israelites complained of lack of food and God heard their cry, "they looked toward the wilderness, and the glory of the Lord appeared in the cloud" (Exod. 16:10). On Mount Sinai, when Moses went up to speak to God, "the cloud covered the mountain. The glory of the Lord settled on Mount Sinai. . . .Now the appearance of the glory of the Lord was like a devouring fire on the top of the mountain" (Exod 24:15-17).

Later, when a tabernacle had been prepared (also called the "tent of meeting"), "Then the cloud covered the tent of meeting, and the glory of the Lord filled the tabernacle" (Exod 40:34). Here notice the parallelism: cloud-glory/tent-tabernacle. When the temple had been completed and dedicated under Solomon, "A cloud filled the house of the Lord; . . . the glory of the Lord filled the house of the Lord" (1 Kgs 8:10-11) just as it had done with tent/tabernacle.

With reference to the temple, the glory of God frequently appears in the visions of Ezekiel. The "glory of God" leaves the temple because it has been polluted by sin (Ezek 10-11); but later, in the new and restored temple, the "glory of God" will return and take up residence once again (Ezek 43:1-5).[11]

The "glory of God" is the manifestation of God's presence in the wilderness, on Mt. Sinai, over the tabernacle/tent, in the temple in Jerusalem. Where God's glory is, God is present in an especially focused way; the cloud both shows us God's presence and also "overshadows" it to protect us from its full force. The halo on the crucifix, like the cloud of God's glory, both overshadows Jesus, subduing his light, and points to him as the place of God's special and focused presence. In John's Gospel (as we will explore more fully in Part Four below), Jesus in fact has replaced the temple as the locus of the "glory of God."[12] Jesus said to Martha at the tomb of Lazarus: "Did I not tell you that if you believed, you would see the glory of God?" (John 11:40).

The Hands/Feet/Side [12]

Blood flows from the hands, the feet and the side of Jesus. The blood from the feet drips down naturally from the holes (whether the black circle represents nails or simply holes is hard to determine). The blood from the hands, however, does not drip directly down, as one would expect according to gravity, but instead runs down Jesus' arms to his elbows, [12a.b] a feature we will comment on below. John's is the only Gospel to mention the piercing of Jesus' side: "one of the soldiers pierced his side with a spear, and at once blood and water came out" (John 19:34).[13] The artist here does not depict both blood and water flowing from Jesus' side, but only blood. This too we will comment on below.

The Garment [13]

The garment around the waist of Jesus is clearly not a simple loin-cloth, much less a mere rag of some kind. It is an elegant garment of white with gold trim. What we have here is a priestly vestment.

In the Old Testament, the priestly garments were to be made of linen and gold; blue, purple and crimson yarns could be used (Exod. 28:5). Among them is a garment called an ephod. The ephod of the high priest is especially ornate (Exod 28:6-14), but all the priests were to wear a linen undergarment (Exod 28:42), also called an ephod (1 Sam. 2:18). Saul, the king, ordered one of his soldiers to kill the priests at Nob. We are told: "Doeg, the Edomite, turned and attacked the priests; on that day, he killed eighty-five who wear the linen ephod" (1 Sam 22:18). [13a] When the ark of the Lord, which had been captured by the Philistines, was returned to Jerusalem, "David danced before the Lord with all his might; David was girded with a linen ephod" (2 Sam 6:14). This indicates that David's ritual dance has a priestly aspect.[14]

In John 17, just before Jesus and the disciples left the last supper room, Jesus offered one last prayer: "And for their sakes I sanctify myself, so that they also may be sanctified in truth" (John 17:19). Since sanctification (or, as sometimes translated, consecration) is a priestly activity, already from the fifth Christian century (Cyril of Alexandria, d. 444), chapter 17 of John's Gospel came to be known as Jesus' (high) priestly prayer.[15] Recent study has argued that throughout John's Gospel, just as Jesus replaces other Jewish religious institutions, he also replaces the high priest.[16] Thus the Jesus of John's Gospel was seen not only as king but also as priest.

A further possible "priestly garment" reference may be noted in the Gospel, but it is not depicted on the cross. The soldiers "also took his tunic (*chiton*); now the tunic was seamless, woven in one piece from the top. So they said to one another, 'Let us not tear it, but cast lots for it to see who will get it'" (John 19:23-24). Since the Jewish writer, Josephus, tells us that the garment (*chiton*) of the high priest was seamless, some scholars have suggested that Jesus is also being depicted as a priest here.[17]

General Comment [14]

Our artist has depicted Jesus, in accord with the Gospel of John, as king [14a,b] and priest, enthroned on the cross. As the "glory of God" in our midst, Jesus looks out peacefully and serenely. [14c,d] Throughout his passion, Jesus, in this Gospel, is in complete control. "I lay down my life. . . .No one has taken it away from me; rather I lay it down of my own accord" (John 10:17-18).

In the garden across the Kidron Valley, Jesus does not kneel and pray in anguish as in Matthew (26:36-46), Mark (14:32-42) and Luke (22:39-46). Rather, when Judas, the soldiers and police come to arrest Jesus, he knows all that is to happen to him. He answers: "I am he," and they all fall back helpless to the ground (John 18:1-6). Before Pilate, we can legitimately ask, "Is Jesus on trial before Pilate, or Pilate on trial before Jesus?" And only when "It is finished" does Jesus bow his head and give up his spirit (John 19:30). He is in control even to the end.

In view of this, is it really accurate to think of Jesus' passion and death, as depicted in the Gospel of John, as a "passion" narrative? The words of Raymond E. Brown here are very apt: "I use the term 'passion narrative' for John as I do of the other Gospels, even though I suspect John would not think of it as a narrative of suffering (passion). For him it would be the narrative of the lifting up of the Son of Man in victorious return to the Father."[18]

The Community under Jesus' Arms [15]

Under Jesus' outstretched arms, are gathered a group of five people, two on the left (as we face the cross) and three on the right. I will argue below that an additional four persons appear, also on the right, for a total of nine. The artist has helped our task by writing the names under the key figures. On the left are Mary and John (*Santa Maria* and *S. Johannes*); on the right, Mary Magdalene and Mary, (mother) of James (*Maria Magdalena* and *Maria Jacobi*), and the Centurion. We will examine these from left to right.

Mary and John [16]

It is only the Gospel of John that mentions Mary and John at the cross (John 19:26-27), but it does not call them by these names. It mentions "his mother" and "the disciple whom he loved." [16a] The only other place Mary appears in this Gospel is at the wedding feast of Cana (2:1-12), and there too she is referred to simply as "the mother of Jesus" (2:1, 3). If all we had was the Gospel of John, we would not know what her name was. This was quickly and easily supplied from the Gospels of Matthew (1:16, 18) and Luke (1:26). And in both places, Jesus addresses her as "Woman" (John 2:4; 19:28), most likely an indication that she is playing a symbolic role, perhaps that of the mother of the new community, the church.[19]

In the Gospel of John, the Beloved Disciple is clearly a very important figure, appearing in six clear references (13:23-26; 19:25-27; 20:2-10; 21:7, 20-23, 24) and perhaps more vaguely in several others (e.g., 18:15; 19:35). While the Gospel itself never makes the identification, the Beloved Disciple has been identified with the apostle John from ancient times.[20]

The Beloved Disciple first appears in the Gospel at the Last Supper, where he is described as "reclining next to him [Jesus]" (John 13:23). The Greek says literally, "was reclining on Jesus' bosom." In the Prologue of the Gospel, Jesus is described as the one "who is close to the Father's heart [literally: in the bosom of the Father], who has made him known" (1:18). As Jesus in the bosom of the Father is the source for our knowledge of God, so the Beloved Disciple on the bosom of Jesus is the primary source for the Johannine community's knowledge of Jesus. Our artist has depicted John (the Beloved Disciple) leaning into the side, the bosom of Jesus

The Two Marys

Crucifixions were intended to be public executions, so the fact that many other people would be standing around and watching was to be expected. All four of the Gospels mention onlookers at the scene, but the reports differ one from another. [17]

- Many women were also there, looking on **from a distance** . . . among them were Mary Magdalene, and Mary the mother of James and Joseph, and the mother of the sons of Zebedee (Mt 27:55-56).
- There were also women looking on **from a distance**; among them were Mary Magdalene, and Mary the mother of James the younger and of Joses, and Salome (Mark 15:40).
- But all his acquaintances, including the women who had followed him from Galilee, stood **at a distance** watching these things (Luke 23:49).
- Meanwhile, standing near the cross of Jesus were his mother, and his mother's sister, Mary the wife of Clopas, and Mary Magdalene (John 19:25).

As we might expect, in the course of the tradition, these various people get mixed up. Mary Magdalene occurs in three of the accounts; Mary of Clopas, who appears only in John, seems to be identified with Mary, the mother of James (Joseph, Salome). [18] The contrast here between John and the other three Gospels is more important than the exact identity of the women. All of the Synoptics indicate that the women are standing at a distance, far off. In John, it is specifically mentioned that they are near the cross. Is John making a particular point here?[21]

The Centurion [19]

Next to the two Marys, a figure in Roman garb appears and is identified as the centurion. John's Gospel does not place the centurion at the cross; perhaps he is being conflated with the centurion mentioned there in the Synoptics (Mt 27:54; Mark 15:39; Luke 23:47). The story of the healing of a centurion's son appears in both Matthew (8:5-13) and Luke (7:1-10). A story with some similarities appears in John 4:46-54 and is designated, in Johannine terminology, as Jesus' second sign at Cana of Galilee (John 4:46, 54). In the Synoptic accounts, the centurion is certainly a Gentile (Mt 8:10; Luke 7:4-5, 9). In John, he is called a "royal official" (*basilikos*) and may, in fact, have been a Jew.[22] Very early, however, from the time of St. Irenaeus (d. ca. 200), these two accounts were being seen as variants of the same story and were blending together.[23]

An indication exists that our artist, in fact, had in mind the version in the Gospel of John. The father realized that his son was cured at the moment when Jesus said to him, "Your son will live." "So he himself believed, along with his whole household" (John 4:53). [19a] This summary phrase appears only in John. Looking over the shoulder of the centurion, we find depicted the face of a young man, his son, and the tops of three heads behind him. [19b] Later in the Gospel, Jesus will say: "I have other sheep that do not belong to this fold. I must bring them also, and they will listen to my voice" (John 10:16).[24] The artist has brought some other sheep—some Gentiles, the centurion, his son and family—who have come to faith in Jesus.

Community of Faith [20]

Assembled under the arms of Jesus enthroned on the cross, we find a community of nine persons: Jesus' mother, the Beloved Disciple, two Jewish women, some Gentiles, a man, his son and family. This is an inclusive community of Jews and Gentiles, women and men, young and the old. We are not far removed here from Paul's famous statement in the letter to the Galatians: "There is no longer Jew or Greek, there is no longer slave or free, there is no longer male or female; for all of you are one in Christ" (3:28; see also 1 Cor 12:13; Col. 3:11).

Two further details can be noted. First, behind this community is a bright light. The theme of Jesus as the Light of world is, of course, a familiar one in John's Gospel. In the Prologue, Jesus is the light of all people; he shines in the darkness; he is the light that enlightens everyone (1:4-5, 9). Later, Jesus will himself affirm: "I am the light of the world" (8:12). The faith community lives in the light of Christ.

Second, we noted above that the blood from Jesus' hands does not drop down naturally, as would be expected from the pull of gravity. Instead, it runs down his arms to his elbows and then drops down into and onto the community of faith. In the "Bread of Life" discourse in John 6, Jesus repeatedly stresses: "Unless you eat the flesh of the Son of Man and drink his blood, you have no life in you. Those who eat my flesh and drink my blood have eternal life . . . for my flesh is true food and my blood is true drink" (6:53-56).[25] In the same way as the blood from his hands, so the blood from the side of Jesus flows out into the community. The inclusive community of faith, protected under his arms, living in his light, is nourished by his blood. [20a]

In commenting on this scene, Raymond Brown stresses that, in John's Gospel, "Jesus reconstitutes the principal members of the third group [i.e. friends and disciples of Jesus at the cross], the mother and the beloved disciple, as a family in discipleship." Jesus' last act on the cross both reveals and brings about a new relationship; Jesus' natural mother is brought into the new family, the community "born from above" (John 3:3), represented by the beloved disciple. "By relating his mother (natural family) to the Beloved Disciple, Jesus has enlarged the discipleship in a significant way as a sign that it will grow and contain many from diverse backgrounds." As we noted above, the women who, in the other Gospels, stand "at a distance," in the Gospel of John stand near to the cross. Brown comments on this: "John's relocation . . . shows that the Son of Man lifted up on the cross has begun drawing all things to himself (John 12:32-34)." Our artist has captured this understanding.[26]

The Smaller Figures at the Bottom, the Sides, and the Top [21]

We now move to the smallest figures on the cross, arranged on the bottom, along the sides and at the top. Here we will start at the bottom and work our way up.

The Bottom [22]

The bottom panel of the crucifix is probably the most difficult to interpret for the simple fact that it is practically all missing. Two male figures with halos are visible on the far right (as we face the cross), but the rest is quite obscure. The bottom of the cross would have been most accessible to those praying before it, and it is most likely that centuries of kissing, touching or rubbing has wiped most of this panel away. Our first reaction when looking at it is simply a question: what could it have depicted? [22a]

Faced with this situation, various scholars have made sugges-
tions as to what might have been there. We can mention four here as
representative:[27] [23]

- St. Damian, St. Rufinus, St. John the Baptist, Sts. Peter
  and Paul, St. Michael? (L. Bracalone)
- The disciples looking up, awaiting the glorious return of
  Christ? (L. Hardick)
- Christians called to be holy; from this position they can
  see Jesus, but imperfectly? (M. Picard)
- The ancestors and holy people of the Old Testament? (R.
  Moriceau)

We can return and look at the panel again with these in mind.
[24, 24a] I have another suggestion to offer for this panel, but first,
let us examine the other small figures. After that we can return to
the question of this bottom scene.

The Rooster [25]

Moving up the right side of the cross, about on a level with Jesus'
knees, we find a small bird with its beak open. [25a] It is easy to see
here a reference to the denial of Jesus by the apostle Peter, an event
mentioned in all four of the Gospels.[28] In John's Gospel, this betrayal
is foretold at the last supper: "Jesus answered, 'Will you lay down
your life for me? Very truly, I tell you, before the cock crows, you
will have denied me three times'" (13:38). This prediction is fulfilled
in John 18:15-18 and 25-27: "Again Peter denied it, and at that moment the cock crowed" (John 18:27).[29] [25b]

The Two Observers [26]

As we continue moving up the cross, we find two figures, one on
the right and one on the left. Their overall stance is the same—hand
on hip, eyes raised up looking at Christ—but their dress and appearance are quite different. The artist has helped us to identify the
figure on the left by writing his name under him—Longinus. The
gospel merely identifies him as "one of the soldiers [who] pierced
his side with a spear" (John 18:34). The Greek word used here for

"spear" is *logche* (pronounced "longke"), and this seems to be the basis for later tradition naming him "Longinus" or "spear-man."[30] Our artist has placed a rather long spear in his right hand. The Gospel of John is the only gospel to mention this piercing of the side of Jesus.

Who then is the other figure, the one on the right? Since all the gospel accounts mention that Jesus was given wine on a sponge to drink (Mark 15:36; Mt 27:48; Luke 23:36; John 19:29), a number of scholars have suggested that this figure is the soldier who gave him the sponge soaked in wine. Very late tradition (tenth century) gives this figure a name as well: Stephaton.[31]

I do not find this identification convincing for several reasons. Since all the other figures here are in fact named, why wasn't he? Conceivably, the artist might not have been familiar with that tradition. But more substantially, the clothing of the Roman Longinus is very similar to that of the Roman centurion. If this figure is also a Roman, why are his garments so different? And if not a Roman, then who? Also, there is no evidence, as far as I can see, of a reed or a sprig of hyssop (John 19:29) with a sponge on it in the figure's hand, nor is there any indication of wine. I think we need to look in another direction.

In John 19:37, we read: "And again, another passage of scripture says, 'They shall look on the one whom they have pierced.'" The scripture reference is to Zechariah 12:10; the relation of the gospel citation to the original Hebrew text is complex and need not detain us here.[32] Our question rather is, who are the "they" which is the subject of the sentence. Again, scholars discuss this;[33] but in the context of our crucifix, I suggest that the "they" refers to the two groups responsible for putting Jesus to death, a death that culminates in his being pierced—the Romans (represented by Longinus) and Jewish leaders (represented by the other figure). [26a] The two look on Jesus who now reigns gloriously from his throne/cross.[34]

The Angels

Jesus was taken down from the cross and buried in a nearby tomb. "Now there was a garden in the place where he was crucified, and in the garden was a new tomb in which no one had ever been laid" (John 19:41). Then, on the first day of the week, on Sunday, some women come to the tomb (Mary Magdalene and the other Mary [Matt. 28:1]; Mary Magdalene and Mary, the mother of James and Salome [Mark 16:1]; the women who had come with him from Galilee [Luke 23:55-24:1]; only Mary Magdalene [John 20:1]).[35] And what do they find there? Each gospel is slightly different. [27]

- And suddenly there was a great earthquake; for **an angel** of the Lord . . . came and rolled back the stone . . . and the angel said . . . (Mt 28:2-5).
- As they entered the tomb, they saw **a young man**, dressed in a white robe, sitting on the right side . . . and he said to them . . . (Mark 16:5-6)
- But when they went in, they did not find the body. While they were perplexed about this, suddenly **two men** in dazzling clothes stood beside them (Luke 24:3-4).
- And Mary . . . saw **two angels** in white, sitting where the body of Jesus had been lying, one at the head and the other at the feet (John 20:11-2).

It is only John's Gospel that mentions two angels being present in the tomb. Our artist has depicted six angels [28] (the two at the ends have their wings folded, the four under the arms have wings extended), but more accurately, three sets of two, all of them pointing to the victorious and glorified Christ. [28a]

The Ascension [29]

Our next scene, above Jesus' head and inscription, shows Jesus ascending into heaven. He is clothed with a golden garment of victory, with a purple scarf of royalty draped over his shoulders. His right leg is lifted slightly as he rises up. His left hand holds a cross on a long shaft, the cross now become his royal scepter, and on his face is a slight smile. He is welcomed back into the heavenly realm by ten angels, five on either side, all of them with wings visible but folded.

The inscription, which we examined earlier as being over the head of Jesus (as indicated in the gospels), can also be read in its context on this crucifix as also being under the feet of Jesus. Just as many of the other smaller figures have their names indicated under them, the inscription tells us that this figure now decked out in the attire of royalty is truly "Jesus of Nazareth, the King of the Jews."

When we think of Jesus' ascension to the Father, we are usually influenced by the approach to this that we find in the Acts of the Apostles, reflected in the liturgy, where the ascension is separated from the resurrection by forty days (Acts 1:3). But this is not the approach of the Gospel of John. In Acts, the ascension is the "levitation symbolizing the terminus of the appearances of the risen Jesus." For John, the crucifixion, resurrection and ascension of Jesus are all together part of one great moment—"the glorification of Jesus in the Father's presence."[36]

To the Father's Right Hand [30]

In the Christology of John's Gospel, Jesus' home is in the heavenly realm with God. "In the beginning was the word, and the word was with God" (John 1:1).[37] This word was sent by God and "became flesh and lived among us, and we have seen his glory, the glory of a father's only son" (1:14). "Indeed God did not send the Son into the world to condemn the world, but in order that the world might be saved through him" (3:17). In his discourse with Nicodemus, Jesus affirms: "No one has ascended into heaven except the one who descended from heaven, the Son of Man" (3:13). At the last supper, Jesus will tell his disciples: "I have come from the Father and have come into the world; again, I am leaving the world and am going to the Father" (16:28).

In understanding the ascension of Jesus, the early Christians drew especially on one verse from the Psalms, Psalm 110:1: "The Lord said to my lord, 'Sit at my right hand until I make your enemies your footstool.'" In fact, this is the psalm verse most used in the New Testament.[38] The risen and ascended Jesus now sits at the Father's right hand. Curiously, this verse is not cited in the Gospel of John where Jesus returns to the bosom of the Father from whence he came. Our artist though has depicted the Father in the form of the Father's right hand, extended as if in blessing.

Some have suggested that the hand of the Father contains additional symbolism. The blessing of God is the Holy Spirit; also, the

Holy Spirit is at times referred to as *digitus paternae dexterae*, the finger of the Father's right hand (in the hymn, *Veni Creator Spiritus*). While this would certainly be appropriate in a Johannine context— Jesus sends the Spirit (e.g., 16:7)—I do not find it completely convincing.[39] From the Carolingian period onward, artists in the West often depicted the ascension with the hand of the Father outstretched to receive Jesus.[40]

Overview of Small Figures [31]

Now that we have looked at each of the small figures—at the bottom, along the sides and at the top of the cross—let us take an overview of what we have seen:

- Bottom????
- Peter, one of the disciples, denies Jesus, before the cock crows
- Jesus is put to death by Jewish and Roman authorities
- Two angels in the empty tomb
- Jesus ascends/returns to the heavenly host
- And to the Father's right hand

We can see fairly easily that, as we look at each figure and then move up the cross to the next one, we are in fact moving progressively through the highlights of the passion narrative of John's Gospel. Each figure is a visual representation that calls to mind key incidents in the passion. We can in fact refer to these small figures as a visual meditation on the passion of John. [31a]

The Bottom Revisited

If this is the key to interpreting these smaller figures, as I believe it is, then we can return to an earlier question [32] and ask it in a different way. Instead of asking simply: "What do I think was depicted in the partially preserved panel at the bottom?" we can focus more sharply and ask: "Where is it likely that the artist began his visual clues for reflection on the passion of John?"

One suggestion might be: the agony in the garden. However, as we noted above, in John's gospel, there really is no "agony" in the garden in the strict sense of the term. Also the episode in the garden was not one of the disciples' better moments; all that is clear in the bottom panel are two figures with halos.

A better guess might be found in noting the overall structure of the Gospel of John. Scholars are in general agreement that the Gospel as a whole can be divided into two main sections. The first is often called The Book of Signs (chapters 1:19-12:50) and the second, The Book of Glory (chapters 13:1-20:31). Others suggest that, between the Prologue and Resurrection accounts, Jesus Reveals God's Glory (1:19-12:50) and Jesus Receives God's Glory (13:1-19:42).[41] Either way, the second main section of the Gospel begins with chapter 13.

If we look at chapter 13, we see that this is the beginning of John's account of Jesus' last supper with the disciples. [32a] Is it possible that what we have in the bottom panel is a Last Supper scene? Certainly a number of figures would be depicted (only two of which survive), and the black object, left-center, could be part of a table. If this were the case, we could note that the blood from the feet of Jesus drips down on this scene, a possible echo of the "unless you drink my blood" theme we noted above, but here in a more explicit Eucharistic context. Once again, certainty is not possible, but, because of the general context of the smaller figures, I find this a more likely guess.

One further observation can be made in this regard. This is not an additional argument, but simply a suggestion. We know from the early sources that, when Francis was very close to death, he was stretched on the earth. Then he asked that something from the gospel be read to him. Thomas of Celano continues the description: [32b]

> Then he ordered the book of the Gospels to be brought in. He asked that the Gospel according to John be read to him, starting with the passage that begins: Six days before the Passover, Jesus knowing that the hour had come for him to pass from this world to the Father . . .[42]

None of the sources say where the reading stopped. Since Francis himself quotes often from John's Last Supper discourse, it is possible it would be at least that much. However, in light of what we have just suggested, we can suggest a certain fittingness—just as Francis began his life of conversion with a visual meditation on John's passion beginning with the Last Supper (?), he would end his life, now almost totally blind, with an aural meditation on the same scene(s). We would have a type of spiritual *inclusio*.

Summary of Conclusions

Here at the end, we might briefly summarize our conclusions about the San Damiano Crucifix and the Gospel of John:

[33] Jesus is depicted as king enthroned on the cross. As the "glory of God" in our midst, Jesus looks out peacefully and serenely. He is also a priest who consecrates, intercedes and sacrifices on our behalf.

[34] Assembled under the arms, the protection, of Jesus enthroned on the cross, we find a community of faith: Jesus' mother, the Beloved Disciple, two Jewish women, a Gentile man, his son and family. This is an inclusive community of Jews and Gentiles, women and men, young and the old. They live in the light of Christ and are nourished by his blood. This is the effect of Jesus' exaltation on the cross.

[35] Each of the small figures along the bottom, sides and top of the cross, is a visual representation that calls to mind key incidents in the passion narrative. They represent and call us to a visual meditation on the passion of Jesus as presented in the Gospel of John. This takes us in narrative fashion (and in a visual sense as well as we move our eyes up the cross) through the events leading up to and including Jesus' crucifixion, resurrection and ascension to the Father's right hand.

[36] The artist has provided us, in visual form, with a rich summary statement of many key themes in the Gospel of John, themes that call out for and repay much reflection and meditation.

[37, 38, 39, 40, 41]

PART THREE
FRANCIS AND THE GOSPEL
OF JOHN[43]

Chapter 23 of the *Earlier Rule* is an extended prayer in which Francis thanks God and calls on all the angels and saints to join him. He prays:

> Because of your love, we humbly beg
> the most glorious Mother, the most blessed,
> ever-virgin Mary,
> Blessed Michael, Gabriel, and Raphael,
> [all the choirs of angels]
> Blessed John the Baptist,
> John the Evangelist,
> Peter and Paul,
> [and all the saints]
> to give you thanks for these things . . . [44]

In the litany of saints that Francis invokes, John the Baptist occupies the first place. This is expected as Jesus had said: "Truly I tell you, among those born of women no one has arisen greater than John the Baptist" (Matt. 11:11). We can also note that John (the Baptist) was Francis's baptismal name, and Celano tells us that Francis would keep this feast more solemnly than the feast of any other saint.[45]

What is not expected is the appearance next of John the Evangelist.

> But what is astonishing is that Francis places John the Evangelist immediately after John the Baptist and ahead of the great apostles Peter and Paul. . . .The precedence accorded to John the Evangelist—is it not significant?[46]

We noted above that, as Francis approached his death, he asked that something from the gospel be read to him. He requested a passage from the Gospel of John, starting with the lines, "Six days before the Passover, Jesus knowing that the hour had come for him to pass from this world to the Father" (John 12:1; 13:1).[47] We do not know how far the reading continued. Some have suggested at least through chapter 17, the so-called "High Priestly Prayer," as this was a favorite of Francis (as we will see below).[48] I suggested above that it might have included the passion as well. What is of interest here is that Francis, in what was almost his last breath, asked that the Gospel of John be read to him.

Statistics?

Several scholars have suggested that statistics showing the number of biblical citations appearing in Francis's writings also point to a preference for the Gospel of John:[49] The use of statistics in this instance, however, suffers from certain limitations.

First, we know from the *Chronicle* of Jordan of Giano (#15) that, when Francis wrote the *Earlier Rule*, he gave it to Brother Caesar of Speyer ("a man learned in the Scriptures") to "adorn it" with words from the gospel. We are thus not always sure if the scripture quotations derive from Francis or from Caesar.

Second, we are not always certain if we are dealing with a scripture citation or not. The text tradition of Francis's writings is not always as clear as we would wish, and this is true even of Cajetan Esser's critical edition. Also, Francis rarely cites texts exactly; rather he quotes freely and from memory, often through association of ideas and key words.[50]

Third, it is not enough simply to count biblical citations to prove the influence of particular Scriptures on Francis's writings. It is not so much the quantity as the quality that is important in giving us a sense of the impact that certain texts had for him. We have to look at a slightly larger picture.[51]

When we turn to this larger picture, the importance of the Gospel of John stands out. Francis's favorite images of Jesus do seem to come from this Gospel, and they are also important in the life of the fraternity he founded.

Favored Johannine Images

In his classic study of Jesus in the writings of Francis, Norbert Nguyen concludes:

> More than half the expressions and images that refer to Christ are derived from the writings of the Beloved Disciple: the Servant who washes the feet, the Lamb, Good Shepherd, Word of the Father, Light, our Lord and Teacher, beloved Son, Brother, the Way, Truth and Life.[52]

Following the order in which they appear in the Gospel of John, we will look at several of these in a little more detail.

The Word of the Father

"In the beginning was the Word, and the Word was with God, and the Word was God" (John 1:1). The Prologue of John's Gospel presents Jesus as the Word (*Logos*) of the Father. The Word has both identity with and distinction from God, and all things were created through him. This Word "became flesh and lived [literally, "pitched his tent"] among us" (1:14). He came from the bosom of the Father to make the Father known (1:18). "The Prologue to the Fourth Gospel is the fullest and clearest statement of incarnational Christology in the New Testament."[53]

The Incarnation of the Word of the Father lies at the heart of the spirituality of Francis of Assisi. He begins the *Second Letter to All the Faithful:*

> I decided to offer you in this letter and message the words of our Lord Jesus Christ, Who is the Word of the Father. . . .The most high Father made known from heaven through His holy angel Gabriel this Word of the Father—so worthy, so holy and glorious—in the womb of the holy and glorious Virgin Mary, from whose womb he received the flesh of our humanity and frailty. Though he was rich, He wished . . . to choose poverty in the world beyond all else.[54]

For Francis, the incarnate Word was the gift to us from the Father's overflowing love. The Word of the Father abandoned his heavenly riches to clothe himself in human poverty. This divine humility is the manifestation of God's love. In his writings Francis is rather restrained in recalling Jesus' earthly life, but he loves to consider the simple fact of the Incarnation and is overwhelmed by the humility of God.[55]

When Francis speaks of the Word of the Father now given to us in the Eucharist, he speaks in a similar way:

> Behold, each day He humbles Himself as when he came from the royal throne into the Virgin's womb; each day He Himself comes to us, appearing humbly; each day He comes down from the bosom of the Father (John 1:18) upon the altar in the hands of a priest.[56]

For Francis, the Eucharist is a continuation of the Incarnation itself and reveals the same "sublime humility" and "humble sublimity." His devotion to the Eucharist impels him to cry out: "Brothers, look at the humility of God."[57]

Francis makes one other reference to the Word of the Father in a text that we might miss if we are unaware of its rich medieval background. In the *Later Rule*, he says:

> I admonish and exhort those brothers that when they preach, their language be well considered and chaste . . . announcing [to the people] vices and virtues . . . with brevity, because our Lord when on earth kept his words brief.[58]

On the surface, this sounds like an exhortation to give short homilies! While there is undoubtedly truth in this, there is much more operating here. The Latin original says, "*quia verbum abbreviatum fecit Dominus super terram*," literally, "because the Lord made an abbreviated [shortened] word upon earth." The phrase is ambiguous: who is the Lord, and what is the word?

If "the Lord" is Jesus, then the "abbreviated word" in his preaching would be the commandment of love of God and of others which sums up all the Law and Prophets (Mt 22:36-39) and his "new commandment" to "love one another as I have loved you" (John 13:34).

But the phrase, "the Lord made an abbreviated word," has a rich background in the spiritual writings of the Middle Ages.[59] Most often "the Lord" is God the Father, and the "word" is Jesus. This is developed by the spiritual writers in two ways. First, in the Old Testament, God spoke many words (*verba multa*), but in the New, God spoke one Word (*verbum unum*), the Word of the Father. So in relationship to the Old Testament, Jesus is the "abbreviated word."

The second understanding reflects a deeper Christological meaning also rooted in the Prologue of John. The Word is present with God for all eternity; he is "in the bosom of the Father" (John 1:18). But when the Word became flesh in the womb of Mary and was born in Bethlehem, the Word gave up his heavenly condition (Phil. 2:6-11) and "abbreviated/shortened" himself, even to the size of a baby in the stable. Thus, in the Incarnation itself, "the Lord made an abbreviated Word." The humility and poverty of this "shortened Word" lie at the center of the spirituality of Francis.

The Lamb

In the Gospel of John, John the Baptist bears witness to Jesus: "The next day he saw Jesus coming toward him and declared, 'Here is the Lamb of God who takes away the sins of the world!'" (John 1:29, 36). Like most of the titles for Christ, this one has multiple meanings.

> By using the title Lamb of God, the Evangelist may mean to say about Christ any or all of the following: (1) He is the symbol of the new Passover [i.e. the Paschal lamb], the new liberation from bondage, offered by God. (2) He is the innocent victim whose suffering and death gain the removal of human sin [sacrificial lamb]. (3) He is the figure who appears at the end of time to destroy all evil in the world [the lamb of the Apocalypse]. (4) He is the servant of God whose suffering atones for the sins of others.[60]

Thomas of Celano tells us that, while Francis overflowed with love for all of God's creatures, "among all the different kinds of creatures, he loved lambs with a special fondness and spontaneous affection, since in Sacred Scripture the humility of our Lord Jesus Christ is frequently and rightly compared to a lamb." Once, while on a journey, he came upon a flock of goats with a little lamb "walking humbly and grazing calmly" among the goats. Deeply touched, Francis said to his companion: "Do you see that sheep walking so meekly among those goats? I tell you, in the same way our Lord Jesus Christ, meek and humble, walked among the Pharisees and chief priests."[61]

But for Francis, the lamb is also a symbol of Jesus' lordship over all. In *The Praises to Be Said at All the Hours,* he inserted as number 3 this praise based on the Book of Revelation 4:11, "The Lamb who was slain is worthy to receive power and divinity, wisdom and strength, honor and glory and blessing."[62] The image of lamb was important for Francis and combines the two aspects of Christ's life, his humiliation and his exaltation.[63]

The Good Shepherd

In the Synoptic Gospels we find passages which compare Jesus' relation to his followers to that of a shepherd and his sheep (e.g., Mt 26:31; Luke 12:32). Perhaps best known is the parable of the lost sheep (Mt 18:10-14; Luke 15:3-7). But it is in John 10 that we find this image developed most fully. Jesus affirms: "I am the good shepherd. The good shepherd lays down his life for his sheep" (John 10:11). The Greek adjective here is *kalos,* which normally means "beautiful." Here it seems to have the nuance of an ideal or model of perfection, so some have suggested translating it as "I am the noble shepherd" or "I am the model shepherd."[64]

For the Johannine community, Jesus alone is the model shepherd. What is most characteristic of his shepherding is not any claim to power and authority over his sheep but rather his intimate knowledge and love for them. Leadership in the community must be measured in the light of the "model." Later, after the resurrection, when Peter is given a role of community leadership, it is expressed in similar terms—he is "to feed and tend the sheep" and be prepared to lay down his life for them (John 21:18-19).[65] It is a leadership that expresses itself further at the Last Supper when Jesus rises and washes the feet of the disciples (see below).

Three times in his writings, Francis explicitly alludes to the Good Shepherd. In *Admonition 6,* he writes: "Let all of us, brothers, consider the Good Shepherd Who bore the sufferings of the cross to save his sheep." In the second version of the *Letter to the Faithful*, he turns again to this image: "O how holy and how loving, gratifying, humbling, peace-giving, sweet, worthy of love, and above all things desirable it is to have such a Brother and such a Son: Our Lord Jesus Christ, Who laid down his life for his sheep." Finally, in the *Earlier Rule*, he urges, "Let us have recourse to Him as to the Shepherd and Guardian of our souls, Who says: 'I am the Good Shepherd Who feeds My sheep and I lay down My life for my sheep.'"[66]

In the last citation, Francis alludes also to a passage from 1 Peter 2:25: "For you were going astray like sheep, but now you have returned to the shepherd and guardian of your souls." Nguyen comments on this:

> This image of Christ guided Francis in his conception of the office of minister general. He must be a good shepherd to his brothers, that is, one who places his life at the service of the brothers and is a good example to them. Francis did not wish the one in charge of the community to be called prior, but minister, servant, guardian, and custodian. We believe that the titles "guardian" and "custodian" are a direct reference to the image of Christ the Good [model] Shepherd.[67]

The One Who Washes Feet

The second part of the Gospel of John, the so-called Book of Glory (chaps. 13-21), begins with Jesus and his disciples gathered at supper. Jesus rises from the table, puts off his outer garment, wraps himself in a towel and washes the feet of his disciples (13:12). It is almost as if he is acting out the words of Luke 12:37: "Blessed are those slaves whom the master finds alert when he comes; truly I tell you, he will fasten his belt and have them sit down to eat, and he will come and serve them." This is an example of humble service, and symbolically characterizes Jesus' impending suffering and death as a work of service. It is, further, an act that the disciples should imitate.[68]

But, as is so often the case with John's gospel, there are other meanings as well. Jesus' action can be seen as an expression of friendship, a friendship based on equality. "By washing his disciples' feet, Jesus overcame by love the inequality which existed by nature between himself and those he had chosen as friends." He is "subverting in principle all structures of domination. . . .The desire for first place has no function in friendship."[69] Further, in the light of hospitality practices at the time of Christ, it can be seen as an act of welcoming his disciples into the household of God.[70]

At the time of Francis, the dominant understanding of Jesus' action would have been that of humble service, and it is in this light that Francis understands it. In addressing brothers who were placed in authority over others, he says:

> I did not come to be served but to serve, says the Lord [Mt 20:28]. Let those who are placed over others boast about that position as much as they would if they were assigned the duty of washing the feet of their brothers. And if they are more upset at having their places over others taken away from them than at losing their position at their feet, the more they store up a money bag to the peril of their soul (Adm 4).

In the Earlier Rule (1221), he urges: "Let no one be called "prior" but let everyone in general be called a lesser brother. Let one wash the feet of the other."[71] The Latin says literally "fratres minores." This would in fact become the name of the First Order, Ordo Fratrum Minorum (= O.F.M.), "Order of Lesser Brothers." We can see that the image of Christ washing the feet of his disciples was an important part of what "lesser brother" meant to Francis.[72]

Jesus' Farewell Prayer

Just before leaving with his disciples to face his suffering and execution, Jesus offers one final prayer and testament (John 17). Throughout, it is addressed to "Father" (vv. 1, 5, 11, 21, 24, 25), and apparently the disciples (then and now) overhear it. Since Jesus prays and intercedes for his followers that they be "sanctified/consecrated" (vv. 17, 19), it has come to be known as Jesus' "high priestly" prayer.[73]

Jesus begins by praying to the Father for himself, that he be glorified, i.e., that the presence of God be manifested through him (vv. 1-5). He then prays for his disciples (vv. 6-19), that the Father keep them in his name (v. 11) and keep them from evil (v. 15) and that they be consecrated/sanctified in the truth (v. 17). Finally he prays for all those in the future who will come to believe (vv. 20-26) that all might be one in the love of the Father and Son (v. 26).[74]

The prayer shows some parallels to the Our Father. It is addressed to the Father (6 times); that God's name might be known (hallowed) (vv. 6, 11, 12, 26); that we be kept from evil (v. 15); and that God be glorified (the equivalent of "your kingdom come"). It also echoes some themes from the Prologue of the Gospel: Jesus' preexistence (v. 5); references to "the word" (*logos*) that was sent into the world (v. 14, 17-18); the rejection that will be met (vv. 14-15); and Jesus' making the Father known (vv. 6, 26). The whole dynamism of the prayer can be expressed in terms of love, the love between the Father and the Son, between the Son and the disciples, and the disciples with one other.

Francis cites this prayer of Jesus four times in his writings: in the two versions of the *Letter to the Faithful*, in the *Earlier Rule*, and in Fragment 1.[75] As a sample, we can cite from the *Second Letter to the Faithful:*

> Holy Father, save in your name those whom you have given me. Father, all those you have given me in the world were yours and you have given them to me. The words that you gave me, I have given to them; they have accepted them and known in truth that I have come from you and they have believed that you have sent me. I pray for them and not for the world; bless and sanctify them. I sanctify myself for them that they may be sanctified in being one as we are one. And I wish, Father, that where I am, they may be with me that they may see my glory in your kingdom.

This is a pastiche of quotations from John 17. What is striking is that

> Francis makes his own the prayers and words of Jesus, praying them in his own name and applying them directly to his penitents and friars. . . . In this way, the prayer of Jesus at the Last Supper becomes the farewell prayer, the spiritual testament of the saint to his friends-penitents-brothers.[76]

Among the aspects of John 17 which influence Francis here, the following are typically cited:[77]

◊ The revelation of the name of the Father, especially as "Holy Father."

◊ The love of the Father given totally to the Son.
◊ The Son reveals, makes the Father known.
◊ The intimate union of Father and Son to which all are called.
◊ The intercommunion in living and acting of the Father, Son and Spirit.
◊ The glory of the Son, rooted in his unity with the Father, in his passion and death.

Conclusion

A number of factors come together to suggest strongly that the Gospel of John played a special role in the thought and spirituality of St. Francis. Following the lead of the study of Norbert Nguyen, we have noted four:[78]

- In his litany of the saints, Francis mentions "John the Evangelist" near the beginning of the list.
- It is reported that Francis, as he approached death, wanted to hear from the Gospel of John.
- In his writings, Francis often cites John, but statistical considerations need to be used with some caution.
- Many of Francis's favorite texts and images of Christ derive from John.

This last is, in fact, the strongest of the arguments, and it becomes even more striking when we note some major images from the Synoptic Gospels (Matthew, Mark and Luke) which Francis does not use, such as the Good Samaritan (Luke 10:29-37), the Prodigal Son (Luke 15:11-32), the Sheep and the Goats (Mt 25:31-40), Dives and Lazarus (Luke 19-31), and the Sermon on the Mount/Plain (Matt. 5-7; Luke 6:20-49).

More texts and Christological images from John could be reviewed, but enough has been shown to establish the importance of John in the thought and writings of St. Francis.

PART FOUR
CREATION AND THE GOSPEL
OF JOHN

In this section, we will examine the theme of creation in the Gospel of John, particularly in the prologue (John 1:1-18). Creation is clearly an important theme in the Franciscan tradition,[79] and we will try to show how Francis's view of creation relates well to the Johannine view.

The Prologue of John's Gospel

The Gospel of John is quite different from the other three gospels, and this difference is evident from the very beginning. Whereas the Gospel of Mark begins with Jesus' baptism in the Jordan and his public ministry, and the Gospels of Matthew and Luke preface this with two chapters of "infancy narratives," the Gospel of John takes us back before creation to the pre-existence of the Word (*Logos*) with God.

> In the beginning was the Word, and the Word was with God, and the Word was God. . . .All things came into being through him, and without him not one thing came into being. . . . [T]he world came into being through him . . . and the Word became flesh and lived among us [literally, "pitched his tent among us"], and we have seen his glory (John 1:1-14).

This exalted vision, coming right at the beginning, is meant to control our reading of the gospel as a whole.[80]

We saw above in Part Three, that the incarnation of the Word lies at the heart of Francis's spirituality. In Part Two, we explored a bit the meaning of "his glory." In this section we want to look more closely at the connection between the incarnation and creation as expressed in the Johannine Prologue.

This is a rich topic that goes well beyond the limits of our present project. Here we want to look at two aspects of the Prologue. A gen-

than jewels, and nothing you desire can compare with her" and "she is a tree of life to those who lay hold of her" for "the Lord by wisdom founded the earth" (Prov 3:15,18, 19). In Proverbs 8, Wisdom sings her own praises:

> The Lord created me at the beginning of his work,
> the first of his acts of long ago.
> When he established the heavens, I was there,
> when he drew a circle on the face of the deep,
> when he marked out the foundations of the earth,
> then I was beside him like a master worker;
> and I was daily his delight,
> rejoicing before him always,
> rejoicing in his inhabited world
> and delighting in the human race (8:22, 27,29b-31).[88]

The great value of Wisdom lies in the fact that she was the first of God's works and then was present with God in and throughout God's creative activity. Beginning with God, Wisdom ends up rejoicing in the created world and delighting to be with the human race. She is a figure of mediation between God and the world.

By the time of Ben Sira (ca. 180 B.C.), the figure of Wisdom developed even further. Sirach (Ecclesiasticus) 24 seems to be inspired by and modeled on the poem in Proverbs 8.[89] Wisdom once again sings her own praises:

> I came forth from the mouth of the Most High,
> and covered the earth like a mist.
> I dwelt in the highest heavens,
> and my throne was in a pillar of cloud.
> Alone I compassed the vault of heaven . . .
> and over every people and nation I held sway.
> Among all these I sought a resting place;
> in whose territory should I abide?
> Then the Creator of all things
> gave me a command,
> and my Creator chose the place
> for my tent.
> He said, "Make your dwelling in Jacob,
> and in Israel receive your inheritance."
> And so I was established in Zion.

First, the world is God's house. We read:

By **wisdom** a house is **built**,
and by **understanding** it is **established**;
by **knowledge** the rooms are filled
with all precious and pleasant riches (Prov 24:34).

This is exactly the same language used earlier in the book to speak of God's creating the universe:

The Lord by **wisdom** founded the earth;
by **understanding** he **established**
the heavens,
by his **knowledge** the deeps broke open
and the clouds drop down the dew (Prov 3:19-20).

In the great hymn of Proverbs 8 discussed above, God's wisdom in creating is personified as the Wisdom Woman (Prov 8:22-31); immediately after this, in Proverbs 9:1, we read a summary statement: "Wisdom has built her house, she has hewn her seven pillars" (see also Prov 14:1). "Her pillars suggest those used to support the roof of a large building . . . or the columns founded upon the earth to hold up the cosmic sky."[95] In Proverbs 8:31, we read that Wisdom was "rejoicing in his inhabited world and delighting in the human race." And in Proverbs 9:2-6, Lady Wisdom sends out her invitation to come for a joyful meal. William P. Brown has described this image as "The World as Wisdom's Playhouse."[96]

Since the Lord created/built the house, the universe, with wisdom and understanding, how are we as humans supposed to live in this house? The psalmist admonishes us: "Unless the Lord builds the house, those who build it labor in vain" (Ps. 127:1). We are urged to seek and to live with wisdom and understanding. "Happy are those who find **wisdom**, and those who get **understanding**" (Prov 3:13). When we do this, we put ourselves in line with God's own creative power and activity. We become (and are called to be) co-creators, co-builders with God. God's wisdom/skill, manifested in the world, the "God-built house," is the model of all "skill in living," of all human wisdom. And for the Christian, to live "with wisdom" is to live with and in the image of Jesus Christ, the Wisdom of God.

Thus far we have restricted our attention to the Old Testament texts, but what about us as Christians? The temple in Jerusalem was destroyed by the Romans in 70 A.D. and has never been rebuilt. Further, Jesus told the Samaritan woman by the well: "The hour is coming when you will worship the Father neither on this mountain nor in Jerusalem" (John 4:21). We do have church buildings and cathedrals. Do these function for us now as surrogate temples?

The fact is, we do have a temple, and it has all of the meaning that we have discussed so far. This is an important theme in the Gospel of John. We can point briefly to two indications:

1) In the prologue, John tells us that the Word, present with God from all eternity, the Word through and with whom all was created (like the Wisdom Woman, Jesus embodies the wisdom of God), "became flesh and 'pitched his tent among us,' and we have seen his glory" (1:14). Israel's tent/tabernacle, pitched in the wilderness, was a foreshadowing of the Jerusalem temple. Tabernacle and Temple have the same symbolism. And, just as the "glory of God," the sign of God's special presence, covered the tabernacle and the temple (Exod 40:34; 1 Kgs 8:10-11), so it is present in Jesus.

2) To make this identification even more explicit, in chapter two, after Jesus cleanses the temple, the Jews are upset and ask: "What sign can you show us for doing this?" Jesus answers them: "Destroy this temple, and in three days I will raise it up." When they misunderstand (a common phenomenon in John's gospel), the evangelist tells us, "he was speaking of the temple of his body" (John 2:18-22).

In John's prologue, we move from the Word with God to creation to temple—the temple that is the flesh of the Word. The incarnate Jesus embodies in himself the meaning and reality of the temple, the place where the presence of God is most concentrated and the place where the full worship of creatures is rendered to God. Some Jewish writers roughly contemporary with the New Testament times show that they realize the cosmic symbolism of the temple. Philo and Josephus "interpret the tabernacle as a symbol of the cosmos and occasionally apply a similar interpretation to the Jerusalem temple."[101]

In the light of this, we can apply what we said above—the temple is a microcosm, and the cosmos is a macro-temple—to Christ: the body of Christ is a microcosm, and the cosmos is a macro-body of Christ. In a real sense, the universe is "the body of Christ." Click on the universe and it is "reduced" to the body of Christ; click on the body of Christ, it "enlarges" to the universe.[102]

In the Gospel of John, the two questions, "How does God create?" and "What does God create?" come together in the incarnate Jesus. He embodies the wisdom of God through and with whom the universe was created. He also embodies the "good/beautiful" work of God, the cosmos-temple-house of creation.

St. Francis and Creation

We can conclude now with some comments on St. Francis in relation to this Johannine vision.

As regards our first question above, Francis does speak once of Jesus as the "Wisdom of the Father," but he does not seem to derive this from biblical wisdom texts.[103] In another of his writings, *A Salutation of the Virtues*, he addresses wisdom as a woman, "Hail, Queen Wisdom," but here too does not seem to derive this from the biblical texts. Rather, the "virtues are addressed in the feminine, particularly as *ladies*. This reflects the chivalrous and courtly mannerisms Francis seemed to appreciate. There seem to be direct links between this piece and such medieval poems as the chansons de geste."[104]

As regards the second question, the meaning of creation, we are on more fertile ground. The question of Francis and creation is a rich one and has already been treated in this Franciscan Heritage Series.[105] Here, in our context, we will make four brief comments.

First, the association of Francis with nature is certainly a well known, if not the best known, aspect of him. However, we can see that, in a real sense, Francis is not really a saint of nature at all. He is a saint of creation. Creation and Creator go together, as they certainly did for Francis. He saw, in and through creatures, the hand of their Creator God.

Second, Francis is overwhelmed by the goodness of the gifts of God. His favorite adjective for God is good, and he cannot say it often enough. On the chartula given to Brother Leo, Francis wrote his *Praises of God*: "You are the good, all good, the highest good"; and in his *Prayer Inspired by the Our Father*: "You Lord, are Supreme Good, the Eternal Good, from Whom all good comes, without Whom there is no good." And in keeping with Genesis 1, in the same breath he affirms that God is beauty, not once but twice.[106]

Third, Francis's favorite response to the goodness of God is praise. In the Bible, praise is the most characteristic response to the blessings of God in creation. Praise calls out to others and focuses on the Giver and the Gift.[107] "Praise the Lord . . . because . . . the Lord has been good to me!" Francis experienced his whole life and everything in it as good gifts of the good God, and he praised. Even when faced with death, he praised God for Sister Death (*Canticle* 12).

Fourth, Francis's best known composition with regard to creation is certainly the *Canticle of the Creatures* written shortly before his death. It reflects in a poetic way Francis's whole relationship with creation. And it is a prayer of praise. The word "Praised be" (Italian, *Laudato*) occurs nine times in the poem.

There is, however, another word that occurs more often; it occurs ten times. It is the Italian word "*per*." This one little word is difficult to translate because there are three possible meanings:

a) It can mean "for, because of," and this would express an attitude of thanksgiving.
b) It can mean "by," expressing a sense of instrumentality or agency.
c) It can mean "through," expressing a deeper sense of seeing God's presence in and through creatures.[108]

Each of these can find support in other writings of Francis as well as in the early sources about him. Each expresses something beautiful, worthy and true. All are at home in the thought of Francis. We do not have one word in English that captures all of these nuances, so we have to make a choice; but we should also keep all the meanings in mind.

Perhaps we can go deeper:

- If Francis **saw** all of creation as God's HOUSE,[109] then perhaps he saw us, everyone and everything in creation, as members of one family, children of the same God and brothers and sisters of each other. He called all creatures brother and sister, and he praised God **FOR** the good gifts which this family was to him.
- If Francis **saw** all of creation as God's TEMPLE, as the place where God's presence could be experienced and where we could respond in reverent worship, then perhaps he might call on all of his family to join him in his prayer so that God might be praised **BY** the whole chorus, just as we saw above in Psalm 148.
- If Francis **saw** all of creation as mediating the BODY of Christ to him, then he might praise God **THROUGH** all creatures.[110]

I am not suggesting that Francis arrived at this only or mainly through meditating on the Gospel of John. But I do believe that he lived and expressed, on a deeply personal level and in a deeply personal way, the vision of John with its roots in the Wisdom Literature of the Old Testament.

And the example of Francis remains a challenge for all of us who try in our own ways to follow him and to live out his vision.

- ◊ If we see and really believe that the world is God's house and we, all people and all creatures, are one family . . .
- ◊ If we see and really believe that the world is God's temple, the place where God is present and where we can respond in praise . . .
- ◊ If we see and really believe that the whole world and all that is in it is truly part of the body of Christ . . .

then what will our behavior look like?

The call of wisdom, incarnated in Jesus of Nazareth, is addressed to us today, for our benefit and that of all of creation:

> Happy are those who find wisdom, and those who get understanding. She is a tree of life to those who lay hold of her (Prov 3:12).

PART FIVE
CONCLUSION

We began our discussion in this booklet with an analogy: spirituality is a question of vision. How do we see things? As Christians, we look at God, the world and ourselves through the lens of Jesus Christ, particularly as presented to us in the New Testament writings. As Franciscans, we look at Jesus through the lens provided by Francis, Clare and the early Franciscan writings. We have tried to show that, in both contexts, the Gospel of John plays an important role.

We could have presented our argument as a movie having a tight dramatic unity running through it. Instead we have chosen to present, as it were, three snapshots taken at different times. Relative to Francis of Assisi, we could designate these as "past, present and future." The San Damiano crucifix is at least one hundred years older than Francis; he came to it as something given him from the past. We then turned to Francis himself and examined things he wrote in his own "present" time and to his contemporaries. Finally, we jumped past the time of Francis, centuries into the future, to draw on some biblical scholarship of our own time. In each snapshot, we saw appearing the reflection of the Gospel of John.

In John, Jesus is the eternal Word who comes down from the bosom of the Father to make God known to us, to show us how God "so loved the world." In the Incarnation, the Word became small, "abbreviated," reduced to our size. Though small in size, this Jesus is the great priest who consecrates his people and the true king who rules from the cross. He is the tent, the tabernacle of God, the place where God dwells most fully and where the "glory of the Lord" is seen.

If the Word is the place where God is most present, he is also the place where true worship is returned to God. Through him, all things were and are created. As the temple of God, Jesus is also a microcosm, a small universe. In him, all of creation is seen to be God's house, God's temple. Likewise, all of creation is, in a real sense, his

43

body. Enthroned upon the cross, he draws all things to himself.

He draws all things, beginning with the family of his followers. Those who follow him are each uniquely gifted with the Spirit, and they form a community of friends, of equals, united in a bond of love which is the Spirit. It is an inclusive community of Jew and Gentile, male and female, young and old. It is a community of "lesser" ones who do not lord it over each other but who are called to imitate Jesus as one who serves, as the good-model shepherd who cares for the sheep. This community is most "the body of Christ" when it gathers in the Eucharist to eat his body and drink his blood. The body of Christ in the bread and wine, the body of Christ that is his family, the body of Christ that is all of creation—all come together as one.

As we look at this Johannine and Franciscan vision, we can be moved, enriched and illumined. But that is ultimately not enough. We are to be transformed by it so that others may also come to see and enjoy this vision as well. And for better or worse, the lens that they have is the witness of our own lives.

Endnotes

[1] As a good introduction, see Frank J. Matera, *New Testament Christology* (Louisville, KY: Westminster John Knox Press, 1999); he treats the Johannine material in chapter 6, "The Revelatory Word," pages 215-42.

[2] *Opuscula Sancti Patris Francisci Assisiensis*, ed. K. Esser, O.F.M. (Rome: Grottaferrata, 1978).

[3] For some references, see footnote 43 below.

[4] For a brief introduction to the question of icons, see Kallistus Ware, "The Spirituality of the Icon," in *The Study of Spirituality*, ed. C. Jones *et al.* (Oxford University Press, 1986), 195-98.

[5] See Thomas J. Herbst, O.F.M., *The Humanization of Christ in the Central Italian Panel Crucifixes of the Twelfth and Thirteenth Centuries Reflected in the Development of Franciscan Christology*, Master of Arts Thesis (Berkeley, CA: Graduate Theological Union, 1989).

[6] Our project here is limited to examining this Johannine dimension. The cross could also be studied with benefit from other angles, e.g., the artistic. In his commentary on the cross, Marc Picard, O.F.M.Cap., for example, gives some attention to the style and color of the garments [*The Icon of the Christ of San Damiano* (Assisi: Casa Editrice Francescana, 1989), 26-28]. A good introduction to these questions can be found in Solrunn Nes, *The Mystical Language of Icons*, 2nd ed. (Grand Rapids, MI: Wm. B. Eerdmans, 2005).

[7] The numbers in square brackets refer to slides in the PowerPoint presentation on the accompanying CD-Rom. For more details, see the Appendix.

[8] 2C 10, *FA:ED* 2, 249; L3C 13, *FA:ED* 2, 76; LMj 2:1, *FA:ED* 2, 536.

[9] For a more complete discussion of the inscription, see Raymond E. Brown, S.S., *The Death of the Messiah*, Anchor Bible (New York: Doubleday, 1994), vol. 2, 962-68. Since this work has a full discussion of many issues relative to the Passion of Christ, we will refer to it often. Two of the letters in the inscription have Greek forms—the second letter (H), which is a Greek E [thus IHS represent the first three letters of the name IESUS], and the third letter of Nazarenus (Z).

[10] Behind the head of Jesus, in the halo, is a Byzantine style cross. I would like to thank both William Short, O.F.M., and Ramona Miller, O.S.F., who personally inspected the cross in Assisi for me and verified that this "halo-in-front" is indeed painted on and not a reflection or shadow produced by photography.

[11] On the glory of God, see Walter Eichrodt, *Theology of the Old Testament*, 2 vols. (Philadelphia: Westminster, 1961, 1967); see vol. 2, 29-35; D.D. Gewaltny and R.W. Vunderink, "Glory," *Eerdmans Dictionary of the Bible*, ed. D. N. Freedman (Grand Rapids, MI: Wm. B. Eerdmans Publishing Co., 2000), 507-509; re. John, see Robert Kysar, *Preaching John* (Minneapolis, MN: Fortress Press, 2002), 143-44.

[12] "Jesus answered them, 'Destroy this temple and in three days I will raise it up.'. . .But he was speaking of the temple of his body" (John 2:19, 21).

[13]See Brown, *Death of the Messiah* 2, 1176-82.

[14]On priestly garments, see Philip King and Lawrence Stager, *Life in Biblical Israel* (Louisville, KY: Westminster John Knox, 2002), 151. Also, Douglas R. Edwards, "Dress and Ornamentation," *Anchor Bible Dictionary* (1992), vol. 2, 234.

[15]Scholars today question how appropriate this title is; see Brown, *Gospel of John* 1, 747-48; George R. Beasley-Murray, *John*, The Word Biblical Commentary 36 (Waco, TX: Word Books, 1987), 204. We will see in Part Three below that John 17 was a favorite of Francis.

[16]See John Paul Heil, "Jesus as the Unique High Priest in the Gospel of John," *CBQ*, 57 (1995): 729-45.

[17]See Brown, *Death of the Messiah* 2, 955-58.

[18]Brown, *Death of the Messiah* 1, 33, footnote 45. More briefly, see Brown's discussion in *A Crucified Christ in Holy Week* (Collegeville, MN: The Liturgical Press, 1986), 68-71; see further, Robert Kysar, *John: The Maverick Gospel*, rev. ed. (Louisville, KY: Westminster John Knox Press, 1993), 49-54.

[19]On this complex question see Brown, *Death of the Messiah* 2, 1020-21; *Gospel of John* 1, 99, 107-109; 2: 922-27. Not all, however, accept this; see, e.g., Beasley-Murray, 348-50.

[20]Few mainstream scholars today would accept this identification. On the issues relating to the identity of the Beloved Disciple, see R. E. Brown, S.S., *The Community of the Beloved Disciple* (New York: Paulist Press, 1979), 31-34 and a briefer summary in his posthumous *An Introduction to the Gospel of John*, ed. Francis J. Moloney, SDB, Anchor Bible Reference Library (New York: Doubleday, 2003), 190-91; Beasley-Murray, lxx-lxxv.

[21]For more discussion, see Brown, *Gospel of John* 2, 904-906; *Death of the Messiah* 2, 1013-19; Beasley-Murray, 348-49.

[22]For discussion on this point, see Robert J. Karris, O.F.M., *Jesus and the Marginalized in John's Gospel*, Zacchaeus Studies: New Testament (Collegeville, MN: The Liturgical Press, 1990), 54-72.

[23]See Brown, *Gospel of John* 1, 192-93; Beasley-Murray, 71.

[24]It is commonly recognized that the "other sheep" refer to the Gentiles. See Brown, *Gospel of John* 1, 396; Beasley-Murray, 171.

[25]For this Johannine theme, see Joseph A. Grassi, "Eating Jesus' Flesh and Drinking His Blood: The Centrality and Meaning of John 6: 51-58," *Biblical Theology Bulletin*, 17 (1987): 24-30.

[26]Brown, *Death of the Messiah*, citations from vol. 2, 1019, 1021, 1026.

[27]See Leone Bracaloni, O.F.M., "Il prodigioso Crocifisso che parlo a S. Francesco," *Studi Francescani*, 11.36 (1939): 203; Lothar Hardick, O.F.M., cited in Optato Van Asseldonk, O.F.M.Cap, "Il Crocefisso di San Damiano visto e vissuto da S. Francesco," *Laurentianum*, 22 (1981): 458; Picard, *The Icon of the Christ of San Damiano*, 34-36; Richard Moriceau, O.F.M.Cap., "Le Christ de Saint-Damien: Commentaire de l'icone," *Evangile aujourd'hui* 131 (August, 1986): 39.

[28]For fuller discussion of these passages, see Brown, *Death of the Messiah* 1, 587-626.

[29]Picard denies this connection since "the icon shows Christ glorified with his chosen ones; the time of denials is past" (*Icon*, 33). As will become clearer below, I

believe this takes the rooster out of its context among the smaller figures on the cross.

[30]This name appears in various manuscripts of the apocryphal Acts of Pilate (copies made in the 5th and 6th centuries); see Brown, *Gospel of John* 2, 935.

[31]Brown, *Death of the Messiah* 2, 1148, note 15. For this identification of the figure, see Van Asseldonk, "Il crocefisso," 458; Octavian Schmucki, O.F.M.Cap., "The Passion of Christ," *Greyfriars Review,* 4 (Supplement, 1990): 44.

[32]For discussion see Brown, *Gospel of John* 2, 938, n. 37; *Death of the Messiah* 2, 1186-88; Beasley-Murray, 355.

[33]See Brown, *Gospel of John,* 954-56; *Death of the Messiah* 2, 1186-88; Beasley-Murray, 355.

[34]Robert J. Karris, O.F.M., has raised the question (oral communication): "Could the figure be the Jewish Nicodemus?" If this were the case, we would have the centurion (conflated with the centurion of the Synoptics) and Nicodemus as figures of faith in Christ. While an intriguing suggestion, the question of whether Nicodemus was considered in the tradition to have been present at the cross needs further study.

[35]Brown, *Death of the Messiah* 2, 1016.

[36]Quotations are from Brown, *Gospel of John* 2, 1012, citing the work of Pierre Benoit, OP; Brown discusses this further on pages 1011-17. See also, Kysar, *Maverick Gospel,* 41-43, 52-53.

[37]"Word of the Father" is a favorite image of Francis. See above, Part Three, page 23.

[38]See among others Matt. 22:44; Mark 14:62; 16:19; Luke 22:69; Acts 2:34-35; 7:55; Rom. 8:34, Eph. 1:20; Col. 3:1. For a helpful discussion of the psalm and its use in the New Testament, see James L. Mays, *Psalms,* Interpretation Commentary (Louisville, KY: John Knox Publishing, 1994), 350-55.

[39]Van Asseldonk also has reservations (*"Non e impossibile, anche se meno probabile"*) "Il crocefisso," 457. For more positive acceptance, see Picard, *Icon,* 38-40; Moriceau, "Le Christ de San-Damien," 35.

[40]Nguyen, *The Teacher,* 100.

[41]For the former, see, e.g., Brown, *Gospel of John* 1, cxxxviii; for the latter, Kysar, *Maverick Gospel,* 18.

[42]1C 110, *FA:ED* 1:278. Thomas of Celano seems to have had a slight slip of memory here; the first words begin chapter 12:1, but the continuation is from 13:1 and it seems almost certain that chapter 13 is meant.

[43]On this topic, the work of Norbert Nguyen-Van-Khanh, O.F.M., *The Teacher of His Heart,* is foundational. Nguyen's work first appeared in French in 1973 and was revised somewhat for an Italian translation in 1984. The English translation is based on this 1984 edition. In addition, some other basic works are the following: Optatus van Asseldonk, O.F.M.Cap. "San Giovanni Evangelista negli Scritti di S. Francesco," *Laurentianum,* 18 (1977): 225-55; "Altri Aspetti Giovannei negli Scritti di S. Francesco," *Antonianum,* 54 (1979): 447-86; "Favored Biblical Teachings in the Writings of St. Francis of Assisi," *Greyfriars Review,* 3 (1989): 287-314, especially pp. 295-305; Thaddée Matura, O.F.M., "How Francis Reads and Interprets Scripture" in *The Gospel Life of St. Francis of Assisi Today* (Chicago, IL: Franciscan Herald Press, 1980), 31-44; Frederic

Manns, O.F.M., "Francisco de Asis, Exegeta," *Selecciones de Franciscanismo* 23 8 (1979), 205-24; this is revised somewhat in "François d'Assise et l'Ecriture," *La vie spirituelle*, 136 (1982): 487-513; James P. Scullion, O.F.M., "The Writings of Francis and the Gospel of John," in *Franciscans and the Scriptures: Living in the Word of God*, Washington Theological Union Symposium Papers 2005, ed. Elise Saggau, O.S.F. (St. Bonaventure, NY: Franciscan Institute Publications, 2006). An important and detailed study of Francis's use of John 13-17 (the Last Supper discourses), Walter Viviani, *L'Ermeneutica di Francesco d'Assisi, indagine alla luce di GV 13-17 nei suoi scritti* (Rome: Antonianum, 1983), was not available to me.

⁴⁴ER 23:6, *FA:ED* 1, 83.

⁴⁵2C 1:3, *FA:ED* 2, 241-3. Celano goes on to apply Matt. 11:11: just as, among those born of women, none is greater than John the Baptist, so among all the founders of religious communities, none is more perfect than Francis.

⁴⁶Nguyen, *The Teacher*, 223.

⁴⁷See Part Two, note 34. 1C 110, *FA:ED* 1, 278; LMj 14:5, *FA:ED* 2, 643.

⁴⁸Nguyen, *The Teacher*, 22.

⁴⁹Nguyen, *The Teacher*, 220; Manns, "Exegeta," 207. See also Matura, "How Francis Reads and Interprets Scripture," 31-44, but he focuses on only four of Francis's writings: the two *Rules*, the *Rule for Hermitages*, and the *Testament*.

⁵⁰Van Asseldonk, "Favored Biblical Teachings," 289-90. See further Robert J. Karris, O.F.M., *The Admonitions of St. Francis: Sources and Meanings* (St. Bonaventure, NY: The Franciscan Institute, 1999), 278-79; 281-300.

⁵¹Van Asseldonk, "Favored Biblical Teachings," 289.

⁵²Nguyen, *The Teacher*, 223-24. See also, Manns, "Exegeta," 208-209.

⁵³Kysar, *Maverick Gospel*, 34. We will take a closer look at the Prologue in Part Four below.

⁵⁴2 LtF 3-5, *FA:ED* 1, 45-46. Here he also alludes to Luke 1-2 and 2 Cor. 8:9.

⁵⁵Nguyen devotes a whole chapter (chapter 3) to developing these ideas (*The Teacher*, 91-110).

⁵⁶Adm 1:16-18, *FA:ED* 1, 129. Here Francis probably depends on John as mediated to him through the liturgy; see Karris, *The Admonitions*, 30.

⁵⁷LtOrd 27-28. *FA:ED* 1, 118. Nguyen, *The Teacher*, 106, 108, 159-64. In analyzing *Admonition 1* (on the Eucharist), Nguyen sees a "decisive" Johannine influence (pages 163-64); Karris, *The Admonitions*, 40-41, is more cautious in this regard.

⁵⁸LR 9:3, *FA:ED* 1, 105.

⁵⁹Henri De Lubac, SJ, *Exégèse Médiévale: Les Quatres Sens de L'Ecriture*, Seconde Partie I (Paris: Aubier, 1961), 181-97; Manns, "Exegeta," 219-20; "François d'Assise et l'Ecriture," 504-505.

⁶⁰Kyser, *Maverick Gospel*, 36. See also, Brown, *Gospel of John* 1, 58-63.

⁶¹1C 77, *FA:ED* 1, 248.

⁶²PrH 3, *FA:ED* 1, 161.

⁶³Nguyen, *The Teacher*, 52.

⁶⁴Brown, *Gospel of John* 1, 386.

⁶⁵R. E. Brown, *The Churches the Apostles Left Behind* (New York: Paulist Press, 1984), 93-94.

[66]Adm 6:1, *FA:ED* 1, 131; 2 LtF 56, *FA:ED* 1, 49; ER 22:32, *FA:ED* 1, 80.

[67]Nguyen, *The Teacher*, 54. He further observes that this image of the Good Shepherd was not common in the artistic representations of the thirteenth century, so it is likely that Francis did not discover it in his medieval surroundings, but drew it himself from the Scriptures (53). See also Van Asseldonk, "Favored Biblical Teachings," 298. Recent research indicates that Nguyen's conclusion may be slightly overstated as the term "guardian" was not used as a term of authority in the writings of Francis.

[68]Brown, *Gospel of John* 2, 564-72; Sandra M. Scheiders, IHM, *Written That You May Believe: Encountering Jesus in the Fourth Gospel* (New York: The Crossroad Publishing Co., 1999), 167. This appeared originally as "The Footwashing (John 13:1-20): An Experiment in Hermeneutics," *CBQ*, 43 (1981): 81-82. Van Asseldonk, "Favored Biblical Teachings," 298-99.

[69]Schneiders, *Written That You May Believe*, 172-74.

[70]Mary L. Coloe, PBVM, "Welcome into the Household of God: The Footwashing in John 13," *CBQ*, 66 (2004): 400-15.

[71]Adm 4:1-2, *FA:ED* 1, 130; ER 6:3, *FA:ED* 1, 68.

[72]Nguyen, *The Teacher*, 45-46. I.-E. Motte, O.F.M., also highlights the connection between the meaning of "friars minor" and the washing of the feet in John in "Se Llamaran 'Hermanos Menores,'" *Selecciones de Franciscanismo* 12 (1975): 274-80. In this same vein, Brown observes (*The Churches*, 88 n. 128): "Because it is so sacred, the eucharist has been very divisive in Christian history. . . . Would Christians have argued with each other so fiercely over the washing of the feet?"

[73]See above Part Two, notes 15 and 16.

[74]For a brief but solid introduction to this rich chapter, see Robert Kysar, *John*, Augsburg Commentary on the New Testament (Minneapolis: Augsburg, 1986), 254-65 and *Preaching John*, Fortress Resources for Preaching (Minneapolis: Fortress, 2003), 210-14.

[75]1 LtF13-19, *FA:ED* 1, 42; 2 LtF 56-60, *FA:ED* 1, 49; ER 22:41-55, *FA:ED* 1, 81; 1 Frg 27-28, *FA:ED* 1, 89. The two versions of the *Letter to the Faithful* are now identified in *FA:ED* 1 as the *Earlier* and *Later Exhortations*; the date and the order of their composition is not settled.

[76]Van Asseldonk, "Favored Biblical Teaching," 302 and the works cited there; see also "San Giovanni Evangelista," 229-34; "Altri Aspetti Giovannei," 471-86. Francis does something similar with prayers to God in his *Office of the Passion* (pointed out to me by Robert J.Karris, O.F.M.).

[77]Van Asseldonk, "Favored Biblical Teachings," 302.

[78]Nguyen, *The Teacher*, 219-24, which summarizes material treated elsewhere throughout the book.

[79]See Ilia Delio, O.S.F., *A Franciscan View of Creation: Learning to Live in a Sacramental World*, Franciscan Heritage Series, vol. 2 (St. Bonaventure, NY: Franciscan Institute Publications, 2003).

[80]See Matera, *New Testament Christology*, 216-18.

[81]R. E. Brown, *An Introduction to New Testament Christology* (New York: Paulist Press, 1994), 205-10; R. Alan Culpepper, "The Christology of the Johannine Writ-

ings," in *Who Do You Say That I Am? Essays on Christology in Honor of Jack Dean Kingsbury*, ed. Mark Allen Powell and David R. Bauer (Louisville, KY: Westminster John Knox Press, 1999), 72-73.

[82]For these and other images, see Walter Brueggemann, *Theology of the Old Testament: Testimony, Dispute, Advocacy* (Minneapolis: Fortress Press, 1997), 145-64; Claus Westermann, *Genesis 1-11* (Minneapolis: Augsburg Press, 1984), 26-41.

[83]The wisdom literature of the Old Testament includes, in their order in the Roman Catholic canon, Job, Psalms, Proverbs, Ecclesiastes (also known as Qoheleth), Song of Songs, the Book of Wisdom (also known as Wisdom of Solomon), and The Book of Sirach (also known as Ecclesiasticus).

[84]See my "Images of God in the Wisdom Literature," *The Bible Today*, 38 (2000): 223-27.

[85]See Westermann, *Genesis 1-11*, 166; "A craftsman has completed a work, he looks at it and finds that it is a success" (p. 113).

[86]For a good introduction to this important issue and the literature associated with it, see Roland E. Murphy, O. Carm., *Tree of Life: An Exploration of the Wisdom Literature*, 3rd ed. (Grand Rapids, MI: Wm. B. Eerdmans, 2002), 133-49, 227-29, 278-81. See also Kathleen O'Connor, "Wisdom Literature and Experience of the Divine," in *Biblical Theology: Problems and Perspectives* (Nashville, TN: Abingdon, 1995), 183-95.

[87]See Murphy, 134-35; Leo G. Perdue, *Wisdom and Creation: The Theology of the Wisdom Literature* (Nashville, TN: Abingdon Press, 1994) 184-86.

[88]A number of words in this text are subject to different interpretations. See Murphy, 135-39; Perdue, 84-93; William P. Brown, *The Ethos of the Cosmos: The Genesis of Moral Imagination in the Bible* (Grand Rapids, MI: Wm. B. Eerdmans, 1999), 271-77.

[89]See Murphy, 140: "Ben Sira obviously wrote the twenty-fourth chapter under the influence of Proverbs 8."

[90]A similar identification of Wisdom and Torah can be found in Baruch 4:1-2. See Murphy, 140-42. For more on Wisdom and the Law, see John J. Collins, *Jewish Wisdom in the Hellenistic Age*, Old Testament Library (Louisville, KY: Westminster John Knox Press, 1997), 42-61.

[91]The Gospel of John is not the only place in the New Testament where this identification is made. The great hymn in Colossians 1:15-20 makes a very similar point. On this see Robert J. Karris, O.F.M., *A Symphony of New Testament Hymns* (Collegeville, MN: Liturgical Press, 1996), 63-91. (On pp. 84-86, Karris connects this hymn with the *Canticle of Creatures* of St. Francis; see further below).

[92]For some theological development of this, see Elizabeth A. Johnson, "Jesus, the Wisdom of God: A Biblical Basis for Non-Androcentric Christology," *Ephemerides Theologicae Lovanienses*, 61 (1985): 261-94, and the later development of this in her book, *She Who Is: The Mystery of God in Feminist Theological Discourse* (New York: The Crossroad Publishing Co., 1992), 86-100, 150-69.

[93]We can note here that biblical Hebrew does not have a word that means "universe." Instead, it uses expressions like "the heavens and the earth" or "all/the totality."

[94]Brown, in *The Ethos of the Cosmos*, explores five such images and their ethical implications: (1) Cosmic Sanctuary (Priestly material of the Pentateuch); (2) Garden (Yahwist material of the Pentateuch); (3) Yahweh's Victory Garden (Second Isaiah); (4) Wisdom's Playhouse (in Proverbs); and (5) Job's Carnival of Animals in the wilderness (Job). To these we could add a sixth, the world as God's Kingdom (Psalms).

[95]Perdue, 95. On pillared houses in ancient Israel, see Philip J. King and Lawrence E. Stager, *Life in Biblical Israel*, Library of Ancient Israel (Louisville, KY: Westminster John Knox Press, 2001), 28-35.

[96]Brown, *Ethos*, 271-316.

[97]For a basic orientation, see Jon D. Levenson, "The Temple and the World," *Journal of Religion*, 64 (1984): 275-98; see also his *Creation and the Persistence of Evil: The Jewish Drama of Divine Omnipotence* (San Francisco, CA: Harper and Row, 1988), 78-99.

[98]There is considerable study of the connections between the creation account of Genesis 1 and the building of the tabernacle (temple) in the wilderness in Exodus 25-40. See among others, Brown, *Ethos*, 73-89; Samuel E. Ballentine, *The Torah's Vision of Worship*, Overtures to Biblical Theology (Minneapolis: Fortress, 1999), 136-42; Terence E. Fretheim, *Exodus*, Interpretation Commentary (Louisville, KY: John Knox Publishing, 1991), 264-78.

[99]There are those who see temple symbolism in Proverbs 9 as well. See Perdue, 95-97; W. P. Brown, *Character in Crisis: A Fresh Approach to the Wisdom Literature of the Old Testament* (Grand Rapids, MI: Wm. B.Eerdmans, 1996), 40.

[100]See the brief but pertinent remarks of Raymond C. Van Leeuwen on Proverbs 9 in "The Book of Proverbs," *New Interpreter's Bible*, 5 (Nashville, TN: Abingdon, 1997), 101-102. We need to note here that the Bible is well aware that there is folly in the house and sin and uncleanness in the temple. The images of creation it presents represent God's ultimate purposes and stand in judgment on any here-and-now situation.

[101]See Craig R. Koester, *The Dwelling of God: The Tabernacle in the Old Testament, Intertestamental Jewish Literature, and the New Testament*, CBQMS, 22 (Washington, DC: The Catholic Biblical Association, 1989), 59-63. He discusses John's Gospel on pp. 100-15; Levenson, "The Temple and the World," 284-85. For a full development of this theme, Jesus as the Temple/Tabernacle of God, see Mary L. Coloe, PBVM, *God Dwells With Us: Temple Symbolism in the Fourth Gospel* (Collegeville, MN: Liturgical Press, 2001).

[102]This raises the question: in the Eucharist, at the time of communion, we hear, "The Body of Christ." How exactly do we think of that? It is the Eucharistic bread; it is the whole Christian community; it is also the whole of the cosmos. If it is any less, then our "body of Christ" is too small. In his study of the Eucharist, *Models of the Eucharist* (New York: Paulist Press, 2005), Kevin Irwin begins with the "Cosmic Mass," as this is the basis of all sacramentality (pp. 39-66).

[103]2 LtF 67, *FA:ED* 1, 50. See Nguyen, *Teacher*, 121-23. Francis's use of texts from the wisdom literature is actually quite sparse and quite general. See my "Old Testament Wisdom Literature, Creation, and St. Francis," in *Franciscans and the Scrip-*

tures: Living in the Word of God, Washington Theological Union Symposium Papers, 2005, ed. Elise Saggau, O.S.F. (St Bonaventure, NY: Franciscan Institute Publications, 2006).

[104]Regis J. Armstrong, O.F.M.Cap., and Ignatius C. Brady, O.F.M., *Francis and Clare: The Complete Works,* Classics of Western Spirituality (New York: Paulist Press, 1982) 151, n. 2.

[105]See Delio, *Franciscan View of Creation;* also, Kenan B. Osborne, O.F.M., *The Franciscan Intellectual Tradition: Tracing Its Origins and Identifying Its Central Components,* Franciscan Heritage Series, vol. 1 (St. Bonaventure, NY: Franciscan Institute Publications, 2003), 63-67.

[106]BlL 3, *FA:ED* 1, 109; PrOF 2, *FA:ED* 1, 158; BlL 4-5, *FA:ED* 1, 109.

[107]For a popular introduction to the meaning of praise in the Bible, see my "The Book of Psalms: Prayers for Everyday Living," *St. Anthony Messenger,* 112.8 (January 2005): 13-16.

[108]See *FA:ED* 1, 114 note a. This translation chooses "through."

[109]We recall that at the beginning of his conversion, Jesus had spoken to him from the San Damiano cross: "Francis, go repair my house. . . ." *FA:ED* 2, 76, 249, 536.

[110]This idea would be unpacked theologically by St. Bonaventure in his principle of exemplarism. See Delio, *A Franciscan View of Creation,* 21-31; *Simply Bonaventure: An Introduction to His Life, Thought, and Writings* (New York: New City Press, 2001), 54-66. Also, Zachary Hayes, O.F.M., "Bonaventure: Mystery of the Triune God," in *The History of Franciscan Theology,* ed. Kenan B. Osborne, O.F.M. (St. Bonaventure, NY: The Franciscan Institute, 1994), 72-9.

APPENDIX
GUIDE TO THE CD-ROM
PRESENTATION

The CD-Rom that accompanies this volume of the Franciscan Heritage Series contains a PowerPoint presentation to illustrate Part Two: The San Damiano Crucifix and the Gospel of John. The numbers in square brackets, e.g., [1], refer to the particular slide; if there are additional clicks to be made on each slide, it is designated by the small letters a, b, c and d. The slides at the beginning [2-5] and end [37-41] of the presentation are meant to take us into and then lead us out of the little chapel of San Damiano where St. Francis meditated on this cross.

[1]		Title
[2]		Coming up the Hill . . .
	[2a]	To the Little Church of San Damiano
[3]		In front of the Church
[4]		Inside the Church, Looking to the Altar
	[4a]	Highlighting the Cross
[5]		St. Francis Praying before the Cross (Giotto)
[6]		The San Damiano Cross
	[6a]	Syro-Byzantine style
	[6b]	Date
	[6c]	Cloth on wood
	[6d]	Dimensions
[7]		The Three Parts of the Study

BIBLIOGRAPHY

Armstrong, Regis J., O.F.M.Cap. and Ignatius C. Brady, O.F.M., eds. *Francis and Clare: The Complete Works.* Classics of Western Spirituality. New York: Paulist Press, 1982.

Armstrong, Regis J., O.F.M.Cap., J.A. Wayne Hellman, O.F.M.Conv., and William J. Short, O.F.M., eds. *Francis of Assisi: Early Documents.* 3 vols. New York: New City Press, 1999, 2000, 2001.

Ballentine, Samuel E. *The Torah's Vision of Worship.* Overtures to Biblical Theology. Minneapolis: Fortress, 1999.

Beasley-Murray, George R. *John.* The Word Biblical Commentary, 36. Waco, TX: Word Books, 1987.

Bracaloni, Leone, O.F.M. "Il prodigioso Crocifisso che parlo a S. Francesco." *Studi Francescani,* 11.36 (1939): 203.

Brown, Raymond E., S.S. *A Crucified Christ in Holy Week.* Collegeville: The Liturgical Press, 1986.

___. *An Introduction to New Testament Christology.* New York: Paulist Press, 1994.

___. *An Introduction to the Gospel of John.* Anchor Bible Reference Library. Ed. Francis J. Moloney. New York: Doubleday, 2003.

___. *The Churches the Apostles Left Behind.* New York: Paulist Press, 1984.

___. *The Community of the Beloved Disciple.* New York: Paulist Press, 1979.

___. *The Death of the Messiah.* Anchor Bible. New York: Doubleday, 1994.

___. *The Gospel According to John I-XII.* Anchor Bible, 29. Garden City, NY: Doubleday, 1966.

___. *The Gospel According to John XIII-XXI,* Anchor Bible, 29A. Garden City, NY: Doubleday, 1970.

Brown, William P. *Character in Crisis: A Fresh Approach to the Wisdom Literature of the Old Testament.* Grand Rapids, MI: Wm. B. Eerdmans, 1996.

Brown, William P. *The Ethos of the Cosmos: The Genesis of Moral Imagination in the Bible.* Grand Rapids, MI: Wm. B. Eerdmans, 1999.

Brueggemann, Walter. *Theology of the Old Testament: Testimony, Dispute, Advocacy.* Minneapolis: Fortress Press, 1997.

Collins, John J. *Jewish Wisdom in the Hellenistic Age*, Old Testament Library. Louisville, KY: Westminster John Knox Press, 1997.

Coloe, Mary L. P.B.V.M. *God Dwells With Us: Temple Symbolism in the Fourth Gospel*. Collegeville, MN: Liturgical Press, 2001.

___. "Welcome into the Household of God: The Footwashing in John 13." *CBQ*, 66 (2004): 400-15.

Culpepper, R. Alan. "The Christology of the Johannine Writings." *Who Do You Say That I Am? Essays on Christology in Honor of Jack Dean Kingsbury*. Ed. Mark Allen Powell and David R. Bauer. Louisville, KY: Westminster John Knox Press, 1999.

De Lubac, Henri, S.J. *Exégèse Médiévale: Les Quatres Sens de L'Ecriture*, Seconde Partie. I. Paris: Aubier, 1961.

Delio, Ilia, O.S.F. *A Franciscan View of Creation: Learning to Live in a Sacramental World*. The Franciscan Heritage Series. Vol. 2. St. Bonaventure, NY: Franciscan Institute Publications, 2003.

___. *Simply Bonaventure: An Introduction to His Life, Thought, and Writings*. New York: New City Press, 2001.

Edwards, Douglas R. "Dress and Ornamentation." *Anchor Bible Dictionary* (1992). Vol. 2. 234.

Eichrodt, Walter. *Theology of the Old Testament*. 2 vols. Philadelphia: Westminster, 1961, 1967.

Esser, Kajetan, O.F.M., ed. *Opuscula Sancti Patris Francisci Assisiensis*. Rome: Grottaferrata, 1978.

Fretheim, Terence E. *Exodus*. Interpretation Commentary. Louisville, KY: John Knox Publishing, 1991.

Gewaltny, D.D. and R.W. Vunderink. "Glory." *Eerdmans Dictionary of the Bible*. Ed. D. N. Freedman. Grand Rapids, MI: Wm. B. Eerdmans Publishing Co., 2000. 507-9.

Grassi, Joseph A. "Eating Jesus' Flesh and Drinking His Blood: The Centrality and Meaning of John 6:51-58." *Biblical Theology Bulletin*, 17 (1987): 24-30.

Guinan, Michael D., O.F.M. "Images of God in the Wisdom Literature." *The Bible Today*, 38 (2000): 223-27.

___. "Old Testament Wisdom Literature, Creation, and St. Francis." *Franciscans and the Scriptures: Living in the Word of God*. Washington Theological Union Symposium Papers, 2005. Ed. Elise Saggau, O.S.F. St Bonaventure, NY: Franciscan Institute Publications, 2006.

___. "The Book of Psalms: Prayers for Everyday Living." *St. Anthony Messenger,* 112.8 (January, 2005): 13-16.

Hayes, Zachary, O.F.M. "Bonaventure: Mystery of the Triune God." *The History of Franciscan Theology.* Ed. Kenan B. Osborne, O.F.M. St. Bonaventure, NY: The Franciscan Institute, 1994.

Heil, John Paul. "Jesus as the Unique High Priest in the Gospel of John." *CBQ,* 57 (1995): 729-45.

Herbst, Thomas J. O.F.M. *The Humanization of Christ in the Central Italian Panel Crucifixes of the Twelfth and Thirteenth Centuries Reflected in the Development of Franciscan Christology.* Master of Arts Thesis. Berkeley, CA: Graduate Theological Union, 1989.

Irwin, Kevin. *Models of the Eucharist.* New York: Paulist Press, 2005

Johnson, Elizabeth A. "Jesus, the Wisdom of God: A Biblical Basis for Non-Androcentric Christology." *Ephemerides Theologicae Lovaniense,* 61 (1985): 261-94.

___ *She Who Is: The Mystery of God in Feminist Theological Discourse.* New York: The Crossroad Publishing Co., 1992.

Karris, Robert J., O.F.M. *A Symphony of New Testament Hymns.* Collegeville: Liturgical Press, 1996.

___. *Jesus and the Marginalized in John's Gospel.* Zacchaeus Studies: New Testament. Collegeville, MN: The Liturgical Press, 1990.

___. *The Admonitions of St. Francis: Sources and Meanings.* St. Bonaventure, NY: The Franciscan Institute, 1999.

King, Philip J. and Lawrence E. Stager. *Life in Biblical Israel.* Library of Ancient Israel. Louisville, KY: Westminster JohnKnox Press, 2001.

Koester, Craig R. *The Dwelling of God: The Tabernacle in the Old Testament, Intertestamental Jewish Literature, and the New Testament. CBQMS,* 22. (Washington, DC: The Catholic Biblical Association, 1989): 59-63.

Kysar, Robert. *John.* Augsburg Commentary on the New Testament. Minneapolis: Augsburg, 1986.

___. *John: The Maverick Gospel.* Rev. ed. Louisville, KY: Westminster John Knox Press, 1993.

___. *Preaching John.* Fortress Resources for Preaching. Minneapolis: Fortress, 2003.

Levenson, Jon D. *Creation and the Persistence of Evil: The Jewish Drama of Divine Omnipotence.* San Francisco, CA: Harper and Row, 1988.

___. "The Temple and the World." *Journal of Religion,* 64 (1984): 275-98.

Manns, Frederic, O.F.M. "Francisco de Asis, Exegeta." *Selecciones de Franciscanismo* 23.8 (1979): 205-24.

___. "François d'Assise et l'Ecriture." *La vie spirituelle,* 136 (1982): 487-513.

Matera, Frank J. *New Testament Christology.* Louisville, KY: Westminster John Knox Press, 1999.

Matura, Thaddée O.F.M. "How Francis Reads and Interprets Scripture." *The Gospel Life of St. Francis of Assisi Today.* Chicago, IL: Franciscan Herald Press, 1980.

Mays, James L. *Psalms.* Interpretation Commentary. Louisville, KY: John Knox Publishing, 1994.

Moriceau, Richard, O.F.M.Cap. "Le Christ de Saint-Damien: Commentaire de l'icone." *Evangile aujourd'hui* 131 (August, 1986): 39.

Motte, I.-E., O.F.M. "Se Llamaran 'Hermanos Menores.'" *Selecciones de Franciscanismo* 12 (1975): 274-80.

Murphy, Roland E., O. Carm. *Tree of Life: An Exploration of the Wisdom Literature.* 3rd ed. Grand Rapids, MI: Wm. B. Eerdmans, 2002.

Nes, Solrunn. *The Mystical Language of Icons.* 2nd ed. Grand Rapids, MI: Wm. B. Eerdmans, 2005.

Nguyen Van-Kanh, Norbert, O.F.M. *The Teacher of His Heart: Jesus Christ in the Thought and Writings of St. Francis.* Franciscan Pathways Series. St. Bonaventure, NY: The Franciscan Institute, 1994.

O'Connor, Kathleen. "Wisdom Literature and Experience of the Divine." *Biblical Theology: Problems and Perspectives.* Nashville, TN: Abingdon, 1995.

Osborne, Kenan B., O.F.M. *The Franciscan Intellectual Tradition: Tracing Its Origins and Identifying Its Central Components.* Franciscan Heritage Series. Vol. 1. St. Bonaventure, NY: Franciscan Institute Publications, 2003.

Perdue, Leo G. *Wisdom and Creation: The Theology of the Wisdom Literature.* Nashville, TN: Abingdon Press, 1994.

Picard, Marc, O.F.M.Cap. *The Icon of the Christ of San Damiano.* Assisi: Casa Editrice Francescana, 1989.

Schmucki, Octavian O.F.M.Cap. "The Passion of Christ." *Greyfriars Review,* 4 (Supplement, 1990): 44.

Schneiders, Sandra M., I.H.M. *Written That You May Believe: Encountering Jesus in the Fourth Gospel.* New York: The Crossroad Publishing Co., 1999. Originally "The Footwashing (John 13:1-20): An Experiment in Hermeneutics." *CBQ,* 43 (1981): 81-82.

Scullion, James P., O.F.M. "The Writings of Francis and the Gospel of John." *Franciscans and the Scriptures: Living in the Word of God.* Washington Theological Union Symposium Papers 2005. Ed. Elise Saggau, O.S.F. St. Bonaventure, NY: Franciscan Institute Publications, 2006.

Van Asseldonk, Optatus, O.F.M.Cap. "Altri Aspetti Giovannei negli Scritti di S. Francesco." *Antonianum,* 54 (1979): 447-86.

___. "Favored Biblical Teachings in the Writings of St. Francis of Assisi." *Greyfriars Review,* 3 (1989): 287-314.

___. "Il Crocefisso di San Damiano visto e vissuto da S. Francesco." *Laurentianum,* 22 (1981): 458.

___. "San Giovanni Evangelista negli Scritti di S. Francesco." *Laurentianum,* 18 (1977): 225-55.

Van Leeuwen, Raymond C. "The Book of Proverbs." *New Interpreter's Bible,* 5 (Nashville, TN: Abingdon, 1997): 101-102.

Viviani, Walter. *L'Ermeneutica di Francesco d'Assisi, indagine alla luce di GV 13-17 nei suoi scritti.* Rome: Antonianum, 1983.

Ware, Kallistus. "The Spirituality of the Icon." *The Study of Spirituality.* Ed. C. Jones *et al.* Oxford University Press, 1986. 195-98.

Westermann, Claus. *Genesis 1-11.* Minneapolis: Augsburg Press, 1984.

ABOUT THE AUTHOR

Michael D. Guinan, O.F.M., is a priest of the Franciscan province of St. Barbara, California. He studied Semitic Languages and Literatures at the Catholic University of America, receiving his Ph.D. there in 1972. Since then he has taught Old Testament and Semitic Languages at the Franciscan School of Theology, a member school of the Graduate Theological Union, Berkeley, California. In addition, over the years, he has taught in other schools and programs, e.g., the summer theology program of St. Bonaventure University, New York (1972-1982); St. Patrick's Seminary, Menlo Park, California, (1981-2003); and the Franciscan theology seminary in Manila, Philippines (summers, 1984-1997). He is a contributor to the *New Jerome Biblical Commentary* (Book of Lamentations), the *Collegeville Bible Commentary* (Book of Job) and the *Message of Biblical Spirituality* series, *The Pentateuch*. He has also contributed to the *St. Anthony Messenger* magazine and other publications of St. Anthony Messenger Press: *Catholic Update, Scripture from Scratch* and *Everyday Catholic*. His particular interest is in biblical spirituality, especially the biblical roots of the Franciscan vision.